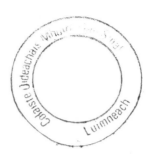

The Search for the Grail

The Search for the Grail

Graham Phillips

CENTURY

First published by Century in 1995

Copyright © Graham Phillips 1995

Graham Phillips has asserted his right under the Copyright,
Designs and Patents Act, 1988, to be identified as the author of this work

First published in the United Kingdom in 1995 by
Century, 20 Vauxhall Bridge Road, London SW1V 2SA

Random House Australia (Pty) Limited
20 Alfred Street, Milsons Point, Sydney
New South Wales 2061, Australia

Random House New Zealand Limited
18 Poland Road, Glenfield
Auckland 10, New Zealand

Random House South Africa (Pty) Limited
PO Box 337, Bergvlei, South Africa

Random House UK Limited Reg. No. 954009
A CIP catalogue record for this book
is available from the British Library

Papers used by Random House UK Limited are natural, recyclable
products made from wood grown in sustainable forests.
The manufacturing processes conform to the environmental
regulations of the country of origin.

ISBN 0 7126 7533 7

Typeset by Deltatype Ltd, Ellesmere Port, Cheshire
Printed and bound in Great Britain by
Mackays of Chatham plc, Chatham, Kent

Acknowledgements

Graham Phillips would like to thank Mark Booth, Lyndsay Symons, Elizabeth Rowlinson, Tracey Jennings, Dan and Susanna Shadrake, Malcolm Ordover, Steven Griffin, Melissa Marshall, Victoria Palmer, Jean Astle, Kerry Harper, Caroline Wise and Steven Wilson for all their invaluable help.

Chapter I

The Holy Grail

And as they were eating, Jesus took the bread, and blessed it, and broke it, and gave it to the disciples, and said, Take, eat; this is my body. And he took the cup, and gave thanks, and gave it to them, saying, drink ye all of it. For this is my blood of the new testament, which is shed for many for the remission of sins.

Matthew 26: 26–8

The Grail has occupied a unique place in the Western imagination since the dawn of the Middle Ages. Even today it remains a central recurring theme in modern literature. It has inspired writers, artists and musicians for centuries, and now it exerts its enchanting influence from the silver screen. A sacred chalice said to hold the power to cure all ills and bring peace and prosperity to the world, the Grail embodies a promise of immortality and the fulfilment of dreams and aspirations.

Over the years the search for the Grail has become as important a motif as the sacred artefact itself. In the literature of the Middle Ages medieval heroes sought the Grail in scores of epic poems and romantic adventures, each gaining worldly insight and spiritual enlightenment from the tasks befalling them during the quest. It became almost unimportant that the Grail itself was not discovered; the real search was for knowledge, and the understanding of the inner self was the true prize. In many medieval stories the Grail was merely a beacon to lure the hero into the ultimate game of life, to discover his true place and purpose in the world. This is the Grail as it was eventually portrayed in the Gothic revival of the nineteenth century, in the paintings of the Pre-Raphaelites and in the verses of the romantic Victorian poets. It is the image that has become the theme of today's novelists and Hollywood scriptwriters. But what exactly is the Holy Grail? Did – or does – it really exist?

The name that immediately springs to mind whenever the Grail is mentioned is King Arthur. So inextricably is it linked with the fabled king – a character widely assumed to be nothing more than myth – that it is generally considered to have been a medieval literary invention. To most people today the Grail occupies the realm of legend. However, during the Middle Ages it was not portrayed simply as another magical artefact, but as the most sacred Christian relic. As such, belief in the Grail's existence was not a matter of profane superstition, but of profound religious faith.

In most medieval Grail romances, from the thirteenth century onwards, the Grail was portrayed as the cup used by Christ himself at the Last Supper, in which the wine became his blood. It was said to have been kept by the disciples during the Roman persecutions, before being brought to Britain, where it was later sought by King Arthur and his knights. Millions of Christians throughout the world firmly believed that Jesus was the son of God and that the miracle of the Last Supper really occurred. From the Christian perspective there was no doubt that the cup of the Last Supper actually existed, and during the Middle Ages many believed that it still survived.

Usually, holy relics were the earthly remains of saints: their bones or, in some cases, a mummified appendage. Relics were believed to hold divine power; they could heal sickness, protect against evil and secure spiritual well-being. In the Middle Ages relics were priceless and highly sought-after, and their acquisition became an international obsession. For many monks it was a sacred duty to seek them out and return them to their abbots. In abbeys throughout Europe relics were displayed in public shrines, to be visited by thousands of pilgrims in the hope that they might be helped, cured or enlightened by their close proximity to the remains. Pilgrims were prepared to pay to view or touch the relics, and vast wealth was donated to the churches, abbeys and cathedrals which contained the bones of the most famous saints. Often a religious centre would grow rich and powerful solely from the proceeds of its relics.

An excellent example is Glastonbury Abbey in Somerset. The impressive ruins of the abbey date from the late twelfth century, replacing much older buildings destroyed by fire in 1184. Following the fire, the abbey was desperately in need of funds for rebuilding, and the only sure way to raise the money was to attract large numbers of pilgrims. In 1190, during renovations to the abbey ruins, the monks claimed to have discovered in the foundations the bones of at least three famous saints: Patrick, Gildas and Dunstan, all thought to be early patrons of the abbey. The relics were put on display and attracted generous donations from multitudes of worshippers. So wealthy did the abbey become that it was reconstructed as one of the most splendid in England.

During the Middle Ages any relics were big business, but the most prestigious were those thought to have been associated with Christ himself. As the Bible relates that Jesus ascended bodily into heaven, his bones could not exist on Earth. It was therefore items associated with Jesus that became his relics. Many splinters from the cross were claimed as genuine, as was the famous Turin Shroud in which Christ's crucified body was said to have been wrapped. If it had survived, however, the holiest of all relics would be the vessel which had once contained the very blood of Christ – the cup of the Last Supper.

The oldest surviving reference to the Grail as the name for the cup of Christ was by the Burgundian poet Robert de Boron, in his *Joseph d'Arimathie*, composed around the year 1200. The Bible relates how Joseph, a rich merchant of Arimathea, laid the body of Christ in the tomb after the Crucifixion. According to Robert, Joseph of Arimathea obtained the cup of the Last Supper from Pilate and used it to collect drops of blood from Jesus' crucified body. In the poem, Joseph eventually embarks on a series of adventures, leading ultimately to the Grail being brought to Britain, to the 'Vales of Avalon'.

In the following decades, other writers composed scores of similar romances, in which the Grail was portrayed as a fabulous jewelled chalice made of gold and silver. If a cup used at an impromptu meal in first-century Palestine really had survived intact, it seems highly improbable that it would be such a spectacular artefact. More likely, it would have been a simple drinking vessel made of wood, stone or pottery. Moreover, it is difficult to equate such an opulent receptacle with Jesus, the humble carpenter who renounced material wealth. So where did the idea of the splendid chalice originate?

Although there is no historical evidence that the cup used at the Last Supper ever survived, the cup said to have been used by Mary Magdalene to collect drops of Christ's blood after the Crucifixion was claimed to have been found in the early fourth century. In 327, after the Roman Emperor Constantine the Great converted to Christianity, his mother, the Empress Helena, ordered an excavation of the presumed site of the Holy Sepulchre, Christ's tomb in Jerusalem. Along with a number of other purported relics, a cup was said to have been found which Helena believed to have been the actual one used by Mary.

Although a number of reliable contemporary accounts do survive of the Empress Helena's excavations of the Holy Sepulchre, there is no historical record of the cup's eventual fate, although the fifth-century Greek historian Olympiodorus wrote that it had been taken to Britain when Rome was sacked by the Visigoths in AD 410. Even if such a cup was genuinely found by Helena, there is no way of knowing on what evidence the empress considered it to have belonged to Mary Magdalene. There are even conflicting stories concerning its appearance: in some it is a small stone drinking vessel, in others it is a larger silver cup, while the most popular tells how it had been incorporated by a Roman craftsman into a splendid gold and jewelled receptacle. Thought to be the most holy relic in Christendom, it was called the Marian Chalice, the Chalice of Mary.

Whether fact or fable, the legends of the Marian Chalice seem to have been the inspiration for Robert de Boron's Holy Grail. The similarity between the Grail as the cup used by Christ, in which the wine became his blood, and the Marian Chalice, in which the blood of Christ was supposedly collected, seems too close a comparison to be mere coincidence. Moreover, according to the writings on the subject, both relics were eventually lost or hidden in Britain.

The importance of the Grail as a religious motif is therefore fairly clear, but what about King Arthur? Why were he and his knights so closely associated with the Grail in the literature of the Middle Ages? For years most scholars have considered the answer to be linked with the medieval crusader knights, in particular the Knights Templar.

The Knights Templar, the most notorious relic-hunters of the Middle Ages, were originally a warrior sect founded in twelfth-century France to fight in the crusades. The crusades began in late eleventh century when the Church decided that Palestine should be captured from the Moslems, ensuring that the land where Christ had lived and taught – the Holy Land – would be in Christian hands. The resultant bloody wars between Christendom and Islam continued on and off for centuries, one side then the other occupying Jerusalem, the sacred city for both religions. The Knights Templar, however, were more than just crusaders, they were Cistercian monks who chose to fight in the Holy Land.

4

The Holy Grail

Throughout the Middle Ages, between campaigns in the Holy Land, many Templars embarked upon journeys in search of holy relics, and these were romanticised in tales first written around 1200. In turn, the tales of Templar quests are generally believed to have inspired the epic stories of Arthur's knights searching for the holiest relic of all, the cup of Christ – the Holy Grail. In many of the romances the guardians of the Grail are actually described as the Templars, for example in Wolfram von Eschenbach's *Parzival* of 1205. Certainly, by the thirteenth century the Knights of the Round Table were firmly associated with the Grail quest in legend and romance. Again, Glastonbury Abbey demonstrates how closely Arthur was linked with the Grail in the public imagination of the time.

Around 1190, the remains of Arthur himself were said to have been discovered at Glastonbury Abbey, along with the bones of the saints. During the excavation of the abbey ruins, the monks claimed to have uncovered a grave containing the bones of a tall man, plus some smaller bones and a scrap of yellow hair. With the remains was a lead cross, said to bear the inscription:

Here lies the renowned King Arthur in the Isle of Avalon.

This inscription was rather convenient, telling the world that not only had Arthur's grave been discovered, but that Glastonbury was the secret island of Avalon, the mystical land of the Arthurian romances. (In early Christian times Glastonbury was surrounded by marshlands, making it virtually an island.)

When the bones were put on display they attracted as many pilgrims as the saints' relics, but the connection with the Arthurian story did not end there. After the appearance of Robert de Boron's Grail poem a few years later, the Grail itself was linked with Glastonbury. In Robert's poem, Joseph of Arimathea took the Grail to Britain to the 'Vales of Avalon'. As the cross inscription supposedly proved that Glastonbury was Avalon, the monks were quick to suggest that the Grail remained to be discovered somewhere in the vicinity of Glastonbury Abbey. Local folklore followed suit and a nearby holy well became linked with the Grail legend. Visiting tourists are still told that it was here that the Grail was originally hidden by Joseph of Arimathea.

However, the Grail legend's connection with Glastonbury is tenuous before the mid thirteenth century. Robert de Boron referred only to

5

Joseph of Arimathea taking the Grail to Avalon, making no reference to Glastonbury by name. In 1247, therefore, the monks decided to rewrite the official history of the abbey, which had been compiled a century earlier by the respected historian William of Malmesbury, in order to couple Joseph, and hence the Grail, with the town. Although William's original treatise on the history of Glastonbury Abbey, *De Antiquitate Glastoniensis Ecclesiae*, written in 1130, mentions nothing of Joseph of Arimathea, the monks' revised version claims that the first church at Glastonbury had been founded by Joseph himself. The myth continued, and to this day the Grail story is still firmly associated in the popular imagination with the town of Glastonbury.

Although the relic-hunting exploits of the crusader knights may have inspired Robert de Boron to write *Joseph d'Arimathea* around the year 1200, the Arthurian story was already linked to the Grail romance. Robert was the earliest known writer to describe the Grail as the cup of the Last Supper; however, he was not the first to record the artefact. A decade before his poem was written, the French poet Chrétien de Troyes included the Grail in his *Le Conte del Graal*, in which Arthur's knight Sir Perceval is cast as the hero who discovers it in the castle of the mysterious Fisher King. Unfortunately, Chrétien not only declines to reveal the castle's location, he also fails to describe what the Grail actually is: he makes no reference to the Last Supper or Joseph of Arimathea.

It seems, therefore, that the Grail may have been associated with the Arthurian story before the romantic tales of the Templars and their quests for holy relics were popularised around 1200. Before we can begin to evaluate the authenticity of any stories which connect the Grail with King Arthur, we must first establish who Arthur was. Was he simply an invention of the medieval imagination? Or did he really exist?

During the Middle Ages, between the twelfth and fifteenth centuries, numerous tales were written about the mighty King Arthur, making Camelot and the Knights of the Round Table famous throughout Europe. Although many themes within these Arthurian romances are clearly invention, a much earlier manuscript – written centuries before these fictional tales were composed – suggests that King Arthur actually did exist. In the ninth-century *Historia Brittonum*, written by the Welsh monk Nennius around the year AD 830, Arthur is recorded simply as the British warrior who defeated the invading Anglo-Saxons at the Battle of Badon, following the Roman withdrawal in the fifth century. According to the eighth-century historian Bede, in his *Ecclesiastical History of the English People*, the Battle of Badon occurred in AD 493, during the Dark Ages, a turbulent period of British history from which few records survive.

As the Battle of Badon was an historical event also recorded by the British monk Gildas, in his *On the Ruin and Conquest of Britain*, written around AD 545 – within living memory of the battle – many historians now accept that Arthur could well have been an authentic British leader who made one of the last effective military stands against the Anglo-Saxons. Furthermore, not only does there appear to have been an historical Arthur, but some of the stories associated with him may also have been based on historical events: the Excalibur legend, for instance, may have originated with an ancient Celtic funerary rite.

The Anglo-Saxons, originally from Germany and Scandinavia, eventually conquered all of England, and the Britons, the native Celts, were driven into what is now Wales. As Arthur had seemingly been a leader of the Britons, legends concerning his deeds appear to have survived mainly in Wales, before inspiring the medieval romances from the twelfth century onwards. The origin of some of the themes within the Arthurian romances of the Middle Ages may therefore be found in early Welsh or Celtic tradition.

The name Excalibur was a lyrical adaptation by the Jersey poet Wace (in his *Roman de Brut*, composed around 1155) of 'Caliburn', the name used for Arthur's sword by the originator of the medieval Arthurian romances, the Welsh cleric Geoffrey of Monmouth, in his *History of the Kings of Britain*, written around 1135. Although it has been suggested that Geoffrey's term derived from the Latin word *chalybs*, meaning steel, Welsh legends indicate another origin. In a number of earlier Welsh tales (for example, *Culhwch and Olwen*, believed to have been composed in the tenth century), Arthur's sword is called Caledfwlch, from the old Celtic word *caladbolg*, meaning 'a flashing sword'. Accordingly, this would imply that the Excalibur theme was taken from an early Celtic tradition.

The familiar story of Arthur's magical sword is not related by Geoffrey of Monmouth, however, who tells us only that it was forged on the Isle of Avalon. It was not until almost a century after Geoffrey that a series of anonymously composed Arthurian tales, known as the Vulgate Cycle, introduced the Excalibur story we know today. In the Vulgate version, Arthur, who originally received Excalibur from a mysterious nymph, the Lady of the Lake, ultimately orders his knight Girflet to cast it into an enchanted pool as he lies dying on the field of battle. After twice disobeying the wishes of his king, the knight reluctantly consents. When the sword is thrown, the arm of the Lady of the Lake rises from the water, catches the weapon by the hilt and takes it down into the crystal depths. Although other romancers cast Bedivere, Lancelot, or even Perceval in this role, the event itself had become firmly entrenched in the saga by the end of the Middle Ages.

There are clear Celtic undertones to the Excalibur theme, suggesting that the writers of the Vulgate story may have been employing much earlier material. Archaeological excavations have unearthed many precious artefacts, including swords, that had long ago been thrown into sacred lakes and pools by the Celtic people of Northern Europe as votive offerings to water deities. One such dig, at Anglesey in 1942, recovered no fewer than 150 items that had been preserved for centuries in the mud of the dried-up lake of Llyn Cerrig Bach. These artefacts were prized possessions, such as cauldrons, horse trappings and brooches, and as such had clearly not been discarded; rather, they had been cast into the water as offerings over a period spanning some 250 years until the end of the first century AD.

The theme of Excalibur being thrown to the Lady of the Lake may therefore have derived from this ancient Celtic practice of making a sacred offering to a water goddess, perhaps from the notion that such an offering might restore the king to health. This hypothesis is further substantiated in the medieval romances, where the Lady of the Lake is given the name Viviane. This name could well have been an adaptation of Covianna, a Celtic water goddess recorded by Roman writers. A shrine to Covianna, under the Romanised name Coventina, can still be seen today on Hadrian's Wall. A well at the shrine has been excavated to reveal numerous votive offerings, particularly coins. From discoveries such as these, it can be deduced that the imperial soldiers stationed in Britain during the Roman occupation (*circa* AD 43–410) began to adopt British customs. Where the British warriors had offered their prized possessions, the Roman soldiers threw coins into the sacred pools, a practice that has survived to this day in the tradition of wishing wells.

The fact that there could indeed be historical truth behind the story of King Arthur and the legend of Excalibur makes it possible that the Arthurian Grail quest may also have been based on some ancient Celtic legend, or even, albeit remotely, on genuine historical events. For this reason we must firstly attempt to place King Arthur more precisely in geographical terms. Did Camelot exist? And if so, where?

Summary

- In most medieval Grail romances, from the thirteenth century onwards, the Grail was portrayed as the cup used by Christ himself at the Last Supper, in which the wine became his blood. It was said to have been kept by the disciples during the Roman persecutions, before being brought to Britain where it was later sought by King Arthur and his knights.

- The oldest surviving reference to the Grail as the name for the cup of Christ was by the Burgundian poet Robert de Boron, in his *Joseph d'Arimathie*, composed around the year 1200. The Bible relates how Joseph, a rich merchant of Arimathea, laid the body of Christ in the tomb after the Crucifixion. According to Robert, Joseph of Arimathea obtained the cup of the Last Supper from Pilate and used it to collect drops of blood from Jesus' crucified body. In the poem, Joseph eventually embarks on a series of adventures, leading ultimately to the Grail being brought to Britain, to the 'Vales of Avalon'.

- Although there is no historical evidence that the cup used at the Last Supper ever survived, the cup said to have been used by Mary Magdalene to collect drops of Christ's blood after the Crucifixion was claimed to have been found in the early fourth century. In 327, after the Roman Emperor Constantine the Great converted to Christianity, his mother, the Empress Helena, ordered an excavation of the presumed site of the Holy Sepulchre, Christ's tomb in Jerusalem. Along with a number of other purported relics, a cup was said to have been found which Helena believed to have been the actual cup used by Mary.

- Although a number of reliable contemporary accounts do survive of the Empress Helena's excavations of the Holy Sepulchre, there is no historical record of the cup's eventual fate, although the fifth-century Greek historian Olympiodorus wrote that it had been taken to Britain when Rome was sacked by the Visigoths in AD 410. There are conflicting stories concerning its appearance: in some it is a small stone drinking vessel, in others it is a larger silver cup, while the most popular told how it had been incorporated by a Roman craftsman into a splendid gold and jewelled receptacle called the Marian Chalice, the Chalice of Mary.

• Whether fact or fable, the legends of the Marian Chalice seem to have been the inspiration for Robert de Boron's Holy Grail. The similarity between the Grail as the cup used by Christ, in which the wine became his blood, and the Marian Chalice, in which the blood of Christ was supposedly collected, seems too close a comparison to be mere coincidence. Moreover, both relics were eventually lost or hidden in Britain. One set of legends was almost certainly based on the other.

Chapter II

The Historical King Arthur

Did the warrior Arthur, as recorded by Nennius writing around the year 830, actually exist? Many scholars refuse to consider the possibility, claiming that the Arthurian romances are just too fanciful. However, Nennius' Arthur is not described in a context of magic and mystery, as he was in the later medieval tales, but in simple historical terms. Nennius is not portraying a romantic Arthur, he is merely writing of a British leader who once fought successfully against the Saxons.

To put into context the role in which Nennius casts Arthur, it is important to understand the fall of the Roman Empire and the resultant backlash in Britain.

In 364 the Roman Empire split into two; the Western Empire was governed from Rome, while the Eastern Empire was centred on Constantinople in what is now Turkey. The early years of the fifth century heralded the end of the Western Empire. Although it struggled on for a few more decades, the imperial establishment had all but collapsed. Its demise began with trouble amongst the Huns of central Asia. Driven at first by a series of disastrous crop failures, these fierce and warlike barbarians surged towards the western Goths, who were in turn driven from their own lands. The vanquished Goths then crossed the Danube and the Rhine, compelling other nations to migrate still further westwards. With Rome on the defensive, the barbarian hordes across Europe began to break through the frontiers of the empire. One barbarian chief, Alaric, King of the Visigoths, reached Italy in 401, and by 408 was laying siege to Rome itself. To meet this challenge, the Romans were forced to withdraw troops from the colonial outpost of Britain.

With the Roman forces severely diminished, it was not long before problems arose on British soil. In the north, the Picts of Scotland began a series of increasingly daring raids across Hadrian's Wall, and in 410 the

British administration appealed for reinforcements from Emperor Honorius in Rome. But the Emperor had troubles of his own, for in the same year Rome itself was sacked by Alaric's Visigoths. Not only did the British receive no reinforcements, but they also lost the legions they still possessed. With the empire in tatters, the Roman army withdrew completely from Britain.

Britain had been part of the Roman Empire for three and a half centuries, the fabric of government long reliant on its military support. This had provided stability for longer than anyone could remember. Now, suddenly, it was gone and anarchy threatened the country. Every freeborn Briton had long been a Roman citizen, and few would have been happy to see the legions leave.

Precise records during this period of British history are few and far between, but an overall picture can be gleaned from St Germanus, the Bishop of Auxerre, who visited Britain in 429 as an envoy of the Catholic Church. According to his biographer Constantius, although there were serious troubles in the north, an organised Roman way of life persisted in the numerous British towns. Even so, matters grew progressively worse once the Roman Empire collapsed altogether in the West.

The tottering empire finally disintegrated in 476 when the German leader, Odovacer, overthrew Emperor Romulus Augustulus and became king of Italy. With all hope of an imperial revival gone, by the late fifth century central administration seems to have collapsed in Britain. In many parts of the country the Britons reverted to tribal allegiances, and regional warlords soon established themselves. With continual territorial squabbles, the island slid inexorably into anarchy and the Dark Ages.

In these troubled times few records were kept, and almost none have survived for us to examine today. The principal reason why so little is known of this period of British history is that the break from Rome removed Britain from the field of the Mediterranean writers, from whom we acquire much of our earlier information. It is, therefore, far from certain exactly what took place in Britain during the fifth century. The basic picture appears to be that the north was suffering repeated incursions from the Picts, while the west was being invaded by the Irish. The greatest problem for the majority of Britons, however, was the struggle for regional supremacy between their own native chieftains. It was into this fragmented country that the Anglo-Saxons began their invasions.

Coastal dwellers from what is now part of Denmark and north

Germany began to cross the Channel to settle in eastern Britain. Rather than attempting to repel these unwelcome Anglo-Saxon migrants, many British chieftains began to enlist their services as mercenaries. Payment included land on which they could settle. By the mid fifth century, however, the Anglo-Saxons were arriving in such large numbers that trouble broke out, and what had begun as a migration soon became an invasion. For some decades the British forces were driven progressively further west, until around 490 when they began to mount a series of successful counteroffensives.

Whoever was commanding the Britons by the last decade of the fifth century was without doubt a formidable leader. The fact that the Britons were stronger and more united than ever before during this period is evidenced not only by Gildas and Bede, but also in archaeology. For example, there were huge dyke fortifications constructed in Lincolnshire and East Anglia. The positioning of the defensive ditch to the eastern side is clear evidence that the dykes were intended to defend against attacks from the east, the Anglo-Saxon side. On the Saxon front there were linear earthworks around the Thames Valley, built by the Saxons to mark a fixed frontier, a defence against the British, who were certainly not the same disorganised rabble routed only a few years earlier. They were now a real threat to the Saxons.

Not only do the massive British fortifications evidence large reserves of manpower, and the Saxon earthworks attest to the Britons having a powerful army, but both these factors suggest a united nation and, more importantly, a strong and determined leader. Was this the warrior Arthur recorded by Nennius?

A chief cause of doubt concerning Arthur's existence is that no contemporary fifth-century record has been found to include his name. However, there survive almost no historical records regarding *any* British leader of the late fifth century, since by that time the country had fragmented into warring factions and law, order and civil administration were almost nonexistent. If Arthur did exist, therefore, the odds are very much against him being found in any contemporary account.

Apart from one or two brief allusions in Dark Age war poems, the oldest surviving reference to Arthur is in Nennius' *Historia Brittonum*, written around AD 830. Although Nennius cannot be cited as absolute proof of Arthur's existence – writing as he was three centuries after the Battle of Badon, in which he tells us Arthur fought – there is nothing in his reference to suggest that Arthur is a fabrication. Introducing a list of Arthur's battles, Nennius says:

> In that time the Saxons strengthened in multitude and grew in Britain. On the death of Hengist, Octha his son passed from the northern part of Britain to the kingdom of the Kentishmen and from him arise the kings of the Kentishmen. Then Arthur fought against them in those days with the kings of the Britons, but he himself was leader of battles.

Everything Nennius associates with Arthur seems to be historically accurate: both of the Saxon warriors he mentions, Hengist and Octha, are referenced in Anglo-Saxon records, and they both lived in the late fifth century, the period in which Nennius places Arthur.

Apart from the surviving writings of a few monks, which mainly concern ecclesiastical matters, the only extant military records covering the late fifth and early sixth centuries were compiled by the Anglo-Saxons. The most important of these is the *Anglo-Saxon Chronicle*, of which a number of copies exist. Although it appears to be based on early West Saxon monastic records, the surviving *Chronicle* was not compiled until the reign of Alfred the Great, between 871 and 899, seemingly under Alfred's personal supervision.

The fact that the *Chronicle* contains no reference to Arthur has long cast a shadow of doubt over his historicity. However, as the work was most likely Alfred's attempt to promote the successful exploits of his own Saxon ancestors, it is reasonable to assume that he would not have wished to draw attention to the accomplishments of the British opposition. In fact, the *Chronicle* provides the names of hardly any British leaders, let alone the successful ones, of whom, according to Nennius, Arthur was one. Consequently, its exclusion of Arthur cannot be used as a conclusive argument against his historical existence.

In support of Nennius, the *Chronicle* does record the Saxon king Hengist. We learn that the Saxon advances into Britain began around the year 455, starting in Kent, and were directed principally by Hengist himself until the 480s. This tallies precisely with Nennius' account, when he refers to Hengist being the Kentish leader shortly before Arthur began to fight the Saxons. In fact, he says that Arthur fought against the Saxons once Hengist had died. The *Chronicle* gives the date of Hengist's death as 488, which would again tally with Arthur's campaigns, if he fought the Battle of Badon in 493.

According to the *Chronicle*, by the time Hengist died much of the south and east of Britain was in Anglo-Saxon hands. This fits with the archaeological evidence, which shows that front-line fortifications were being occupied by the Saxons as far west as the city of Bath. Indeed, it seems to have been at Bath that the Battle of Badon was fought. The city's modern name is derived from its famous Roman baths. The Saxons knew it as Badanceaster, which in turn may have come from the original British word for a bath – *baddon* – which is still preserved in modern Welsh.

The archaeological evidence shows that by the end of the fifth century, the Saxons were in retreat for a few decades, which further sits with the evidence of a major British victory at the time of the Battle of Badon. The fact that the *Chronicle* fails to record the battle at all again demonstrates how its compilers chose to leave unrecorded the British successes of the time.

As Nennius says that Octha had succeeded Hengist by the time Arthur was active, we can assume that it was Octha against whom Arthur fought. Again, Octha was an actual historical figure. A ninth-century Saxon manuscript known as the *Cotton Vespasian*, now in the British Library, offers a list of the kings and bishops of the Dark Ages, including Octha, whom it records succeeding his father Hengist. As Nennius' dating is consistent with the *Chronicle*, and the two other warriors he names along with Arthur appear to have been authentic, there seems no compelling reason to doubt his reference to Arthur being the most important British leader around the last decade of the fifth century.

If Arthur lived in the late fifth century, however, he would not have been a medieval king in shining armour, but a Celtic warlord struggling against invasion by the Anglo-Saxons. The reason why he is now portrayed as a medieval-style king is that the writers of the Middle Ages tended to set ancient stories, such as the legends of Greece and Rome, in their own historical context – a context of knighthood and chivalry. If Nennius' Arthur really existed, he and his warriors would have been very different from the Knights of the Round Table. The warlords of the fifth century wore Roman-style armour, and their fortifications were not huge, Gothic castles, but wooden stockades.

Neither was Britain one nation during the fifth century, but was divided into smaller kingdoms. Centuries passed before England and

Wales became countries in their own right. England came into existence once the Anglo-Saxons united into a single nation; while the native Britons – the Celts, who once ruled all of England and Wales – became known as the Welsh (from the Saxon word *weala* meaning 'foreigners'). Consequently, until the mid twelfth century the exploits of Arthur – a Briton – survived mainly in Welsh tales, before being adapted by writers from England, France and Germany into romantic fables of a feudal monarch of the Middle Ages.

So who was this Arthur, seemingly the leader of the Britons at the Battle of Badon in 493? In 1992 Martin Keatman and I published our research into the truth behind the Arthurian legend, in *King Arthur: The True Story*. During our investigations we were not searching for the King Arthur of romantic fiction, but for a possible historical candidate for the warrior recorded by Nennius – a figure upon whom the later legends may have been based.

According to Nennius, Arthur was the British 'leader of battles', presumably the Britons' most powerful figure. Consequently, we began by attempting to ascertain from where the most powerful British leader of the time might have originated. Much previous research into the identity of the historical Arthur had centred on the south-west of England, such as the famous excavations of Cadbury hill fort in Somerset, which local tradition had associated with King Arthur since the sixteenth century. Led by archaeologist Leslie Alcock, the dig uncovered evidence that the fort had been used by British forces around the time of Badon, but found nothing to suggest it had been a base camp for Arthur himself. Many similar hill forts are known to have been used all along the British/Saxon front line as it existed in the late fifth century, and the Cadbury excavations merely demonstrated that this was one such fortification: the elusive Arthur remained undiscovered.

Ultimately, Martin and I concluded that historians may have been looking in the wrong place. In legend, Arthur is said to have been born at Tintagel Castle in Cornwall, ruled from Camelot at Winchester, and was buried at Glastonbury in Somerset. However, Tintagel and Winchester castles were built six centuries after Arthur is believed to have lived, while the discovery of his grave at Glastonbury Abbey in 1190 is widely suspected to have been a medieval hoax to attract pilgrims. At best, as neither the cross nor the bones the monks claimed to have found still survive, it cannot be proved either way. But if Arthur did not originate in the south of England, where was his seat of power?

Unlike Badon, there is no evidence that a place with the name Camelot ever existed. In fact, the first of the medieval romancers make no mention of it at all. The earliest use of Camelot as the name for Arthur's court occurred in *Lancelot*, a poem by Chrétien de Troyes written around 1180, where it appears only once and in passing. Thereafter, the name was adopted by nearly all the romancers. As Chrétien seems to have invented Camelot in the twelfth century, the name itself is unlikely to help in any search for the base camp of a warrior who lived seven centuries earlier. Furthermore, although all the romancers describe in graphic detail the splendid city and its impregnable castle, they fail to specify its whereabouts.

If the historical Arthur was indeed the most powerful leader, it follows that his base would have been the most powerful stronghold. So what was the principal British city at the time of Badon? From the archaeological perspective it appears to have been the Roman city of Viroconium, not in the south or west of Britain but in the Midlands.

During the Roman occupation of Britain the country had been divided into provincial districts known as *civitates*, each founded on existing tribal areas and controlled from an administrative capital. The four principal cities were London, Lincoln, York and Virconium. From Gildas, Bede and the *Chronicle* we know that within half a century of the Roman withdrawal in AD 410, London and Lincoln were overrun by the Anglo-Saxons, while York was sacked by the Picts. Although other major cities, such as Cirencester and Exeter, were relatively safe from attack, it was Viroconium which appears to have assumed the greatest importance.

Unlike London, Lincoln and York, which are still thriving cities, all that now remains of Viroconium are its ruined walls, standing in quiet farmland outside the Shropshire village of Wroxeter, five miles to the south-east of Shrewsbury. The visible ruins of Viroconium are the remains of a large bathhouse complex erected around AD 150; the ancient brickwork which still dominates the site, known locally as the 'Old Work', was once the south wall of a large aisled basilica that acted as an exercise hall for the baths themselves. Standing as they do in the open countryside, the ruins of Viroconium have provided an excellent opportunity for excavation, and in the last century much archaeological work has been conducted. Today the dig is open to the public and a small museum stands at the site, where some of the excavated material is on display, although the majority is housed in Rowley's House Museum in Shrewsbury.

In the late 1960s, a fresh excavation was initiated at the site. Lasting for well over a decade, it unearthed remarkable evidence that the city remained a highly urbanised administrative capital well after other Roman cities were abandoned altogether. Moreover, it seems that around 420, as other Roman cities were falling into ruins, Viroconium was actually rebuilt.

From the excavation of post holes, and other telltale signs in the foundations and substructure of the city, the fifth-century buildings were found to have been made of timber, not bricks and mortar like those of the earlier Roman town. They were large and elaborate constructions of classical design, with colonnades and orderly façades, many being at least two storeys high. Not only were new buildings erected and streets replanned, but the infrastructure of the city was also repaired. A new drainage system and fresh water supply was installed through an elaborate arrangement of aqueducts, and long stretches of the Roman cobbled roads were completely relayered. The nerve centre of this new Viroconium was a massive winged building constructed on the site of the old basilica. Accompanied by a complex of adjoining buildings and outhouses, this classical mansion appears to have been the palace of a series of important post-Roman chieftains. According to the director of the excavation, Phillip Barker, it may have been one of the last classical buildings to be erected in Britain for another thousand years.

Viroconium is by far the most sophisticated Dark Age settlement yet discovered. Not only does it appear to have been Britain's principal city of the fifth century, it seems to have remained so until well after the Battle of Badon. Accordingly, its palatial mansion was probably the seat of the Britons' most important leader. In other words, if Arthur really existed then Viroconium is the best contender for his power base – the historical Camelot.

Summary

- During the Middle Ages, between the twelfth and fifteenth centuries, numerous tales were written about the mighty King Arthur, making Camelot and the Knights of the Round Table famous throughout Europe. Although many themes within these Arthurian romances are clearly invention, a much earlier manuscript – written centuries before

18

these fictional tales were composed – suggests that King Arthur historically existed. In the ninth-century *Historia Brittonum*, written by the Welsh monk Nennius around the year AD 830, Arthur is recorded simply as the British warrior who defeated the invading Anglo-Saxons at the Battle of Badon, following the Roman withdrawal in the fifth century.

• According to the eighth-century historian Bede, in his *Ecclesiastical History of the English People*, the Battle of Badon occurred in AD 493. As the battle was an historical event also recorded by the British monk Gildas, in his *On the Ruin and Conquest of Britain*, written around AD 545, many historians now accept that Arthur could well have been an authentic British leader who made one of the last effective military stands against the Anglo-Saxons in the late fifth century.

• In legend, Arthur is said to have been born at Tintagel Castle in Cornwall, ruled from Camelot at Winchester, and was buried at Glastonbury in Somerset. However, Tintagel and Winchester castles were built six centuries after Arthur is said to have lived, while the discovery of his grave at Glastonbury Abbey in 1190 is widely suspected to have been a medieval hoax to attract pilgrims.

• If the historical Arthur had been the most powerful leader as Nennius describes, it follows that his base would have been the most powerful stronghold. From the archaeological perspective this appears to have been the Roman city of Viroconium, now a ruin five miles to the southeast of Shrewsbury. In the late 1960s, an excavation was initiated at the site. Lasting for well over a decade, it unearthed remarkable evidence that the city remained a highly urbanised administrative capital well after other Roman cities were abandoned altogether.

• Viroconium is by far the most sophisticated Dark Age settlement yet discovered. Not only does it appear to have been Britain's principal city of the fifth century, it seems to have remained so until well after the Battle of Badon. Accordingly, it was probably the seat of the Britons' most important leader at the time Nennius tells us Arthur was that leader. In other words, if Arthur really existed, then Viroconium is the best contender for his power base – the historical Camelot.

Chapter III

Tracking the Bear King

Why have you been rolling in the filth of your past wickedness ever since your youth, you bear, rider of many and driver of the chariot of the bear's stronghold . . . ?
Gildas, *On the Ruin and Conquest of Britain*, circa AD 545

This passage, written by an obscure British monk in the mid sixth century, may hold a vital clue to the true identity of the mysterious King Arthur. This was ultimately our conclusion after attempting to identify the most likely British leader at the Battle of Badon – the most powerful British warlord, and hence the most promising candidate for an historical Arthur.

By the sixth century Britain had divided into a number of smaller kingdoms, and around 545 the monk Gildas names the rulers of the most important of these. As this is only a generation after Badon, it is very possible that the most influential of these rulers succeeded the British victor at the battle.

Gildas tells us that the most powerful king was Maglocunus, who is recorded both by Nennius and in the tenth-century *Welsh Annals* (now in the British Library) as the ruler of the kingdom of Gwynedd in north Wales. According to Gildas, Maglocunus had come to power by overthrowing his uncle in battle. In his *On the Ruin and Conquest of Britain*, Gildas scolds Maglocunus, saying:

In the first years of your youth, you crushed the king your uncle and his brave troops with fire, spear and sword.

As Maglocunus was well into middle age by the time Gildas was writing,

20

and is described as a youth when he overthrew his uncle, the event must have taken place some time in the early sixth century. This means that his uncle was almost certainly of the same generation as the Britons who fought at Badon. Indeed, as Maglocunus became the most powerful king after defeating him, the uncle may actually have been the Britons' leader at the battle. Was Maglocunus' uncle therefore the historical Arthur? Unfortunately, Gildas fails to name him. All we can tell is that he appears to have been a valiant leader whom Gildas admired.

Interestingly, this uncle does have something in common with the legendary Arthur. A similar story of internecine strife occurs in the medieval romances, in which Arthur dies when *his* nephew attempts to seize the throne. Although in the romances the name of Arthur's nephew is Modred, was the original legend based on the historical Maglocunus? The possibility was certainly intriguing, so Martin and I searched the surviving records to see if we could put a name to this mysterious uncle.

Another powerful leader referred to by Gildas was Cuneglasus, who ruled a separate but unnamed kingdom at the same time as Maglocunus ruled Gwynedd. Cuneglasus is recorded in a genealogy in the *Welsh Annals*, where he is named as Maglocunus' cousin. Cuneglasus' father might therefore have been Maglocunus' uncle, and the fact that Cuneglasus was a powerful ruler in his own right makes it even more likely that it was his father who was usurped by Maglocunus. In other words, Cuneglasus' father ruled a kingdom which divided into two separate kingdoms after his death – his son directly succeeded him in one, while his nephew seized power in the other.

According to Gildas – the most complete contemporary historical evidence that still exists – the father of Cuneglasus is therefore the most likely candidate for Britain's most powerful ruler during the apparent Arthurian era. But who was he? In the *Welsh Annals* Cuneglasus' father is named as Owain Ddantgwyn. There can be little doubt that this was indeed his name, as four separate Dark Age genealogies also record him thus. Consequently, at first it seemed that the most powerful leader at the time of Badon was not called Arthur after all. Yet if we examine the name Arthur we discover that it may not have been a personal name, but a battle name – a title.

Various scholars have theorised that the name Arthur was a British derivative of the Roman name Artorius. In fact, the notion has become popular since John Heath-Stubbs' twelve-part poem, *Artorius*, was published in 1973, followed shortly afterwards by John Gloag's story

Artorius Rex, published in 1977. Although it has been pointed out that a Roman soldier called Lucius Artorius Castus served as an officer in Britain during the late second century, and that another called Artorius Justus was here in the third century, it does not necessarily follow that Artorius was the original version of the name Arthur. In fact, it seems more probable that the name Arthur was derived from the word *arth*, an old British word – still preserved in modern Welsh – meaning 'bear'.

From a number of sources we know that the British warriors of the Dark Ages used animal battle names – as did the native Americans, with designations such as Crazy Horse, White Eagle and Sitting Bull. Early Dark Age war poems such as the *Gododdin*, accredited to the seventh-century bard Aneirin, tell us that many Dark Age warlords were given the name of an animal in some way typifying their qualities.

The *Gododdin* concerns the fate of a group of warriors from the kingdom of that name in southern Scotland who set out to fight the Anglo-Saxons around the year 600. Two mid-thirteenth-century copies of the poem are preserved in the public library in Cardiff. However, from the style of writing and spelling it is thought to have been composed in the early seventh century. In the poem warriors are described by battle names such as the Hound, the Wolf, and one is even called the Bear. Although this particular warrior lived too late to have been the historical Arthur, the *Gododdin* clearly demonstrates that the name Bear was being used as a battle name by the Britons during the Dark Ages.

Gildas too uses the battle names of the leaders he references. For instance, he calls Maglocunus the Dragon. Significantly, he also calls Cuneglasus the Bear. From what is known of Maglocunus, it seems that these battle names were inherited, as his descendants are known to have continued to use his title of the Dragon. Indeed, his descendants eventually conquered most of Wales, and their emblem is still preserved on the Welsh national flag.

It is possible that Cuneglasus similarly inherited his father's battle name. In fact, Gildas, in the quote with which I began this chapter, suggests just that, implying that Cuneglasus, the Bear, is now in command of a fortress that was already known as the Bear's stronghold. In other words, he had inherited a stronghold from a previous Bear, presumably his father Owain Ddantgwyn.

So Owain, the principal candidate for the British leader at Badon, may well have been called Arth, a name which might easily have been altered to the more lyrical Arthur by the time Nennius was writing three centuries later. Indeed, surviving legends suggest just that. In Cornish folklore the stellar constellation of the Ursa Major, the Great Bear, is called Arthur's Wain or Cart. Moreover, the initiator of the Arthurian romances in the twelfth century, Geoffrey of Monmouth, says that Merlin prophesied the coming of Arthur after seeing a vision of a bear amongst the stars. Both of these legendary references, seemingly coupling Arthur with the Ursa Major constellation, clearly demonstrate that he was associated with a bear long before the romances became popular throughout Europe.

So Owain Ddantgwyn seemed to us the most feasible candidate for an historical Arthur. The historical and archaeological evidence had already suggested Viroconium as the most probable seat of the warrior upon whom the legends of Arthur were based. By the late fifth century Britain had fragmented into a number of smaller kingdoms, and Viroconium became the capital of the kingdom that geographically surrounded it – the kingdom of Powys. Now lending its name to a Welsh county, Powys originally covered much of the west Midlands and central Wales. What we now had to discover was whether Owain Ddantgwyn was the king of Powys. Once more, historical detective work was necessary.

We knew that Owain ruled a kingdom that included Gwynedd in north Wales, as Maglocunus had assumed control of that area after his death. But did Owain's kingdom also include what later became the separate kingdom of Powys? From Gildas we knew that Owain's son Cuneglasus was ruling a kingdom that had broken away from Gwynedd by the mid sixth century. Unfortunately, Gildas neglects to name Cuneglasus' kingdom, mentioning only that it included somewhere he refers to as the 'bear's stronghold'. Was this mysterious fortress a citadel in Powys? Indeed, was the 'bear's stronghold' Viroconium itself?

At the time Gildas was writing, the five most powerful British kingdoms were Gwynedd in north Wales, Powys in central England, Dumnonia in Devon and Cornwall, Gwent in south-east Wales, and Dyfed in south-west Wales. As Maglocunus ruled Gwynedd, and Gildas says that a Constantine ruled Dumnonia and a Vortipor ruled Dyfed, it is most likely that Cuneglasus ruled either Powys or Gwent. Since both these kingdoms seem to have shared borders with Gwynedd, either could geographically have been the second half of the kingdom over which Owain Ddantgwyn had ruled.

The family of Cuneglasus, however, can be most closely linked with the kingdom of Powys through the *Cun* affix in their names. In the early British language, Brythonic, and also in modern Welsh, the Latin syllable pronounced *Cun* is spelt *Cyn*. Indeed, in a number of Welsh genealogies, Cuneglasus is spelt Cynglasus or Cynglas. An early Welsh war poem, *The Song of Llywarch the Old* (now in the Bodleian Library), believed to have been composed around AD 850, names the leader of Powys in the mid seventh century as Cynddylan, whose immediate predecessors were Cyndrwyn and Cynan. The *Welsh Annals* also link the family with Powys in 854, when they record that 'Cynan king of Powys died in Rome'. As no such evidence has been discovered to place Cuneglasus' family in Gwent, it would seem that he was almost certainly a king of Powys.

From the archaeological perspective, the recent work of K. R. Dark, the editor of the *Journal of Theoretical Archaeology*, also associates Cuneglasus with Powys. In his *Civitas to Kingdom*, published in 1994, he not only suggested that Cuneglasus was a Powysian leader, but that Viroconium may have been 'the political centre of the Powysian kingdom in the fifth century'.

So it seems fairly certain that Cuneglasus ruled the kingdom of Powys – but would his father Owain Ddantgwyn previously have ruled the same area? Again the archaeological evidence is compelling. A king bearing the affix *Cun* was buried in Viroconium some time around 480 – seemingly before the reign of Owain Ddantgwyn. At the Viroconium excavation in 1967 a tombstone dating from *circa* 480 was discovered just outside the city ramparts bearing the inscription *Cunorix macus Maquicoline*, 'King Cuno son of Maquicoline'.

Thus it seems likely that Owain Ddantgwyn, the most feasible candidate for Arthur, ruled Powys from the city of Viroconium, the most likely historical seat for the British leader at the time Nennius tells us Arthur lived. In other words, from the archaeological and historical perspectives, Owain ruled from the right place at the right time to have been the Arthur referenced by Nennius.

The Arthur of history would appear to have been an important post-Roman chieftain whose name, within a few centuries of his death, became legendary throughout Britain, the reason apparently being that it was he who made the last effective military stand against the invading Saxons. Perhaps the most intriguing mystery, however, is why a Celtic warrior of the Dark Ages should rise to become such a popular figure of romance in Norman England, six centuries after his death.

The principal reason seems to have been political: King Arthur became a crucial figure in a medieval propaganda exercise. The kings of England, of Norman blood following the defeat of the Saxons at the battle of Hastings in 1066, needed desperately to prove their divine right to govern. At a time of poor communications, more than just armies were required to maintain order; the monarchy needed the support of the Church. Also, the continental Capetian dynasty was repeatedly laying claim to the English throne, further pressuring the Normans to legitimise their rule.

Many Saxon noblemen could rightfully claim descent from the true kings of England, such as Athelstan and Alfred the Great; the Norman aristocrats thus required their own heroic and majestic ancestor. Having grounds to prove succession from the ousted pre-Saxon Celtic warriors – many of whom had fled to France and settled in Normandy during the fifth and sixth centuries – it was to them that they looked. Unfortunately, there was no evidence that any of these could really be titled 'kings' in the medieval sense. The closest contender was the fabled warrior Arthur, and in the early twelfth century the English king Henry I patronised the Welsh cleric Geoffrey of Monmouth to write an 'official' history of Britain which included the golden age of King Arthur.

Unfortunately, by Geoffrey's time almost nothing was known of the historical Arthur; all that remained was little more than fable and legend. From these Geoffrey imaginatively reconstructed the Arthurian era, so setting the stage for the medieval romances that followed.

Much of Geoffrey's account is exaggerated, such as a campaign in which he describes Arthur conquering half of Europe, while other details are completely erroneous, such as the inclusion of fourth-century Roman emperors in Arthur's late-fifth-century life. Geoffrey's most problematic legacy, however, is that he set Arthur's life in the south-west of England – evidently a total fabrication.

According to Geoffrey, Arthur was born at Tintagel Castle on the north coast of Cornwall. The romancers who followed took Geoffrey at face value, and to this day Tintagel is associated with King Arthur in the popular imagination the world over. Anyone who visits the tiny village during the holiday season will find it teeming with sightseers of all nationalities. The ruins of the castle itself stand just outside Tintagel, on what is virtually an island surrounded by foaming sea, linked to the mainland by a narrow ridge of rock.

According to Geoffrey's *Historia*, Arthur's father Uther Pendragon had designs on Ygerna, the wife of Gorlois, Duke of Cornwall. Aided by a magic potion, prepared for him by Merlin the Magician, Uther is transformed for a time into the form of Gorlois, and as such he visits the duke's castle at Tintagel and makes love to the duchess. Thus Arthur is conceived. On the death of Gorlois, Uther makes Ygerna his queen and Arthur is born at Tintagel Castle. Based on little more than Geoffrey's word, the medieval romancers thus set their Arthurian stories in the same area, and local folklore quickly followed suit.

Unfortunately, Arthurian mythology and literature and the New Age movement, to say nothing of the south-west's tourist industry, seem unaffected by the simple historical fact that Tintagel Castle could not have been the birthplace of a warrior who apparently lived in the fifth century. It was only built in the early twelfth century for Reginald, Earl of Cornwall. Geoffrey seems to have concocted the story to please the earl, the wealthy brother of his patron, Robert, Earl of Gloucester. Although it has been suggested, in Geoffrey's defence, that Arthur was born in a castle that previously occupied the site, modern excavations have shown that the promontory at that time was actually the home of an early monastic community.

Hardly any literary evidence pre-dates Geoffrey of Monmouth to tell us where Arthur was thought to have ruled. Luckily, however, the Dark Age war poem *The Song of Llywarch the Old*, composed at least three centuries before Geoffrey's time, does place Arthur in a geographical setting; indeed, it is the oldest known work to do so. Significantly, it links Arthur with the same kingdom in which our research has placed him – the kingdom of Powys. Three hundred years before the first of the romances ever connected Arthur with the south-west of England, this Welsh poem says that the Powys kings were the 'heirs of great Arthur'.

In concluding our search for Arthur, it must be admitted that the evidence for him as an actual historical figure rests almost exclusively with Nennius. However, the Battle of Badon, at which Nennius accredits Arthur with victory, was a genuine historical battle, as it is recorded by Gildas within living memory of the event. Although Gildas fails to name the British leader, an early reference in the *Welsh Annals*, written in 950 – two hundred years before the first of the romances – does record Arthur as the leader at Badon. Although the *Welsh Annals* were written a century after Nennius, and seem to be wrong in their dating of Badon (they give the year as 519), no name other than Arthur's is known to have been associated with the British victor at the battle. Accordingly, from the sketchy evidence that still survives, we had found the most likely candidate for the British leader at the time of Badon – Owain Ddantgwyn – and his seat of power – Viroconium. Thus from a military perspective, unless further evidence is unearthed, Owain Ddantgwyn is the most feasible Arthur yet discovered.

Summary

- Around 545 the monk Gildas names the most important British ruler as Maglocunus, a king who seized power by overthrowing his uncle. As Maglocunus was well into middle age by the time Gildas was writing, and he is described as a youth when he overthrew his uncle, the event must have taken place some time in the early sixth century. This means that the uncle was almost certainly of the same generation as the Britons who fought at Badon. As Maglocunus became the most powerful king after defeating him, the uncle may actually have been the Briton's leader at the time – namely the historical Arthur.

- Maglocunus' uncle is recorded in the *Welsh Annals* as Owain Ddantgwyn. Was he the real King Arthur? The name Arthur probably derived from *arth*, an old British word – still preserved in modern Welsh – meaning 'bear'. Many Dark Age warriors are known to have adopted the name of an animal as a battle name, and Gildas refers to Owain's son Cuneglasus as the Bear. In also describing Cuneglasus as the 'driver of the chariot of the bear's stronghold', Gildas implies that the stronghold had once belonged to someone previously called the Bear – seemingly Owain Ddantgwyn. Accordingly, Owain Ddantgwyn – the most likely candidate for an historical Arthur – may well have been called Arth.

- By the late fifth century Britain had fragmented into a number of smaller kingdoms, and Owain Ddantgwyn seems to have ruled that of Powys. Now lending its name to a Welsh county, it originally covered much of the west Midlands and central Wales. Many of Owain's family bore the distinctive name affix *Cun*, such as his son Cuneglasus, and rulers bearing his affix are recorded as Powysian leaders of the fifth and sixth centuries. During Owain Ddantgwyn's reign the capital of Powys was the city of Viroconium. Accordingly, the most plausible candidate for an historical Arthur ruled from the same location where the archaeological evidence also places the historical Arthur.

- Only one literary reference pre-dating the medieval romances places Arthur in a geographical setting: the Dark Age war poem *The Song of Llywarch the Old* says that the Powys kings were the 'heirs of great Arthur'. Composed around AD 850, this Welsh poem implies that Arthur himself was thought to be king of Powys, three centuries before the first of the romances ever connected him with the south-west of England.

Chapter IV

The Grail Romances

Having gained an historical perspective on the Dark Ages and the period during which Arthur seems to have lived, we turn now to the Middle Ages and the birth of the medieval Arthurian Grail romances. Geoffrey of Monmouth and his contemporaries in the eleventh and twelfth centuries re-created Arthur's life from half-remembered historical events; were the overlapping Grail romances similarly compiled?

The original Grail romances consisted of eight stories written within a period of about thirty years between 1190 and 1220. Although the Grail quest featured in many subsequent Arthurian romances, culminating in the most famous version, by Thomas Malory in the late fifteenth century, any investigation into the birth of the legend must begin with these earliest versions. The first, Chrétien's *Le Conte del Graal*, written around 1190, was followed within ten years by two so-called Continuations of his unfinished story, by anonymous authors. Robert de Boron's *Joseph d'Arimathie* then appeared around 1200, as did an anonymous French romance known as the *Didcot Perceval*. The German *Parzival*, by the epic poet Wolfram von Eschenbach, was composed by 1205. A revised version of the *Didcot Perceval*, called *Perlesvaus*, and two Grail stories in the Vulgate Cycle were the last versions in the series to appear, around 1220.

[Chrétien's *Le Conte del Graal*]

Le Conte del Graal, the last of Chrétien's five Arthurian romances composed somewhere between 1170 and 1190, was left unfinished when he died. Introducing the work, Chrétien says that he obtained the story from his patron Count Philip of Flanders, in the form of a book given to him before Philip left for the crusades.

In the story the hero, Perceval, is introduced as 'Perceval of Wales', a sprightly young warrior who had been brought up by his widowed mother in a forest in Snowdonia. He travels to Arthur's court and trains for knighthood but, because of his naivety, his master Gornemant teaches him to keep quiet and to avoid asking questions. After training, Perceval sets out to return home to visit his mother, but during the journey meets two fishermen who direct him to a mysterious castle. Once inside, he is invited to a banquet held in honour of the castle's lord, a lame old warrior called the Rich Fisher. During the feast Perceval witnesses a strange procession in which he sees the Grail:

> While they were talking of this and that, a squire entered from a chamber, grasping by the middle a white lance ... All present beheld the white lance and the white point, from which a drop of red blood ran down to the squire's hand ... [Perceval] watched this marvel, but he refrained from asking what it meant ... he feared that if he asked, it would be considered rude.

Shortly afterwards:

> A damsel came in with these squires, holding between her hands a graal [Chretien's spelling]. She was beautiful, gracious, splendidly garbed, and as she entered with the graal in her hands, there was such a brilliant light that the candles lost their brightness, just as the stars do as the moon or the sun rises.

Later the Grail is described in greater detail:

> [It was made from] refined gold, and it was set with precious stones of many kinds, the richest and most costly that exist in the sea or in the earth.

Although in awe, Perceval remembers what his master taught him about not asking questions, so refrains from quizzing his hosts concerning the Grail. Eventually, he leaves the castle and cannot again discover its whereabouts. At length, he meets a hermit who explains the significance of what Perceval saw at the castle of the Rich Fisher and tells him of his foolishness in not having asked about the Grail:

'Great was your folly when you did not learn whom one served with the graal. The Rich Fisher was my brother; and his sister and mine was your mother. And believe me that the Rich Fisher is the son of the king who causes himself to be served with the graal. But do not think that he takes from it a pike, a lamprey, or a salmon. The holy man sustains and refreshes his life with a single mass wafer. So sacred a thing is the graal, and he himself is so spiritual, that he needs no more for his sustenance than the mass wafer that comes in the graal. Fifteen years he has been thus without issuing from the chamber where you saw the graal enter.'

Shortly after this encounter the story ends abruptly.

From Chrétien we learn that Perceval is, without knowing it, the grandson of the Rich Fisher, and that he is to inherit the Grail. To do so he must ask the right questions. However, the unfinished work leaves us mystified: what exactly is the Grail? Chrétien neglects to describe the artefact's appearance, merely saying it is made of gold and decorated with precious stones. Indeed, he left many unanswered questions, which two anonymous writers attempted to address within ten years of his death.

The First Continuation

The so-called First Continuation is an anonymous story written in Old French around 1190. It is so named because it is the author's attempt to continue the story where Chrétien left off, and consequently has Gawain taking over the role of the hero. When Gawain encounters the Grail in the Rich Fisher's castle we are given additional information concerning the relic, which in some ways is even more confusing.

Then Gawain saw entering by a door the rich Grail, which served the knights and swiftly placed bread before each one. It also performed the butler's office, the service of wine, and filled large cups of fine gold and decked the tables with them. As soon as it had done this, without delay it placed at every table a service of food in large silver dishes. Sir Gawain watched all this, and marvelled how much the Grail served them. He wondered sorely that he beheld no other servant . . .

Still we cannot tell what the Grail is supposed to be, merely that it seems to hover around the room serving food. We can only assume that it is some form of floating plate. We are, however, told its history.

It is true that Joseph caused it to be made: that Joseph of Arimathea who so loved the Lord all his life, as it seemed, that on the day when he received the death on the cross to save sinners, Joseph came with the Grail which he had caused to be made to Mount Calvary, where God was crucified . . . He placed it at once below his feet, which were wet with blood which flowed down each foot, and collected as much as he was able in this Grail of fine gold.

Strangely, in the same story there is a second object also described as a Grail. This time we are told precisely what it is. When Joseph eventually leaves Palestine, he is accompanied by a companion, Nicodemus, who takes with him the second Grail:

Nicodemus had carved and fashioned a head in the likeness of the Lord on the day that he had seen him on the cross. But of this I am sure, that the Lord God set his hand to the shaping of it, as they say; for no man ever saw one like it nor could it be made by human hands. Most of you who have been at Lucca know it and have seen this Grail . . .

Having left this carved head – the second Grail – at Lucca, Joseph and his companions leave on a long journey.

Joseph and his company prepared their fleet and entered without delay, and did not end their voyage till they reached the land which God had promised to Joseph. The name of the country was the White Land.

This land we learn is somewhere in Britain. When Joseph eventually dies he leaves instructions that the original Grail – the one used to collect Jesus' blood – is to remain in the possession of his direct descendants.

At the end of his life he prayed sweetly that he would consent that Joseph's lineage would be rendered illustrious by the Grail. And thus it befell; it is the pure truth. For after his death no man in the world of any age had possession of it unless he was of Joseph's lineage. In truth the Rich Fisher descended from him, and all his heirs and, they say, Guellans Guenelaus and his son Perceval.

The First Continuation portrays the Rich Fisher and Perceval as direct descendants of Joseph of Arimathea, while the Grail (or at least one of them) once contained the blood of Christ. Neither of these themes was included by Chrétien, so the author may have consulted a separate source, perhaps even the same book that Chrétien obtained from his patron. Alternatively, it might have been pure invention.

Robert de Boron's *Joseph d'Arimathie*

We now come to the story that made the Grail famous: the most popular of all the medieval Grail romances, Robert de Boron's *Joseph d'Arimathie*.

Boron is a village near Montbeliard on the Swiss border, where the author wrote under the patronage of a crusader knight, Gautier de Montbeliard. As Gautier departed for Italy in 1199, and died in a subsequent crusade without returning home, Robert's poem was probably written around the same time (he records in his dedication Gautier leaving home). Unlike the authors of the two Continuations, Robert claimed to have a completely separate source from Chrétien for his Grail story. He claimed it came from the book in which important Christian clerics had 'written the histories and the great secrets which one calls the Grail'.

For the first time we are given specific details about the appearance and origin of the relic, which Robert called 'The Holy Grail'. According to the author, after the Crucifixion, Joseph, who had been a secret follower of Jesus, teams up with another convert, Nicodemus, a Roman officer present at Jesus' death. Together they approach Pilate to request Jesus' body for proper burial. Eventually they succeed, also obtaining the cup that had been used at the Last Supper – the Holy Grail.

Accompanied by Nicodemus, Joseph uses the vessel to collect a few drops of blood from Jesus' body before laying him in the tomb. When, on the third day after the Crucifixion, the Jews discover the body missing, they accuse Joseph of removing it, throw him into prison, and confiscate the sacred chalice. There the resurrected Jesus appears to Joseph in a blaze of light, returns to him the Grail, and tells him he has custodianship of the holy relic. Christ also instructs Joseph in the saying of mass, and informs him that the vessel is to be called the 'calice'. Strangely, however, Robert thereafter refers to it as the Grail.

Joseph is eventually rescued after the sacking of Jerusalem by the Romans in AD 70, and escapes to Britain with his brother-in-law Bron. Bron has a son, Alein, whose own son is Perceval. Each of these men in turn is called the Rich Fisher, the secret title for the one who possesses and protects the Grail. Robert not only provides a complete history of the Grail and fully describes what it is, he even tells us what the word means: it comes, he claims, from the old French word *agree*, meaning to delight or satiate, indicating that the cup provides spiritual refreshment.

Confusion, however, arises over the time scale. If Perceval is the grandson of Bron, Joseph's contemporary in first-century Palestine, how is he alive in the Arthurian era of the fifth century, the period in which Robert places Perceval? The answer is left to the next romancer, the anonymous author of the *Didcot Perceval*, who makes Bron immortal. By the time of Perceval, Bron is centuries old due to the Grail's powers of rejuvenation.

The *Didcot Perceval*

The prose romance *Perceval*, or the *Didcot Perceval* as it is now known, was written some time around 1200. It has survived into modern times in two separate manuscripts, the older found in the *Didcot Manuscript* in the French National Library in Paris. (The word Didcot has nothing to do with the original author, but is the name of a former owner of the manuscript, Firmin Didcot.)

In the manuscript the *Didcot Perceval* is preceded by a prose version of *Joseph d'Arimathie*; it was therefore once thought to have been a prose copy of a lost poem by Robert de Boron. However, on further examination of its style, it now seems that the *Didcot Perceval* is derived from another literary source entirely. Indeed, in the introduction the author claims to have discovered a more authentic source than his predecessors, including even Chrétien de Troyes, the originator of the Grail romances:

> But of this Chrétien de Troyes does not speak, nor the others who have composed of it in order to make their rhymes pleasant, but we tell only so much as appears in the story and as Merlin had written

34

by Blayse his master . . . And he saw and knew the adventures that
happened to Perceval each day, and had them written by Blayse in
order that they may be spoken of to worthy men who would wish to
hear them. Now know what we find in the writings that Blayse
relates to us, just as Merlin made him write down and record it.

So according to the anonymous writer, the story was originally written
by someone called Blayse. The story opens with Merlin explaining to
Arthur the origin of the Round Table:

'It was made to signify the table where Our Lord sat on the
Thursday when he said that Judas would betray him. And also the
table was made after that of Joseph which was fashioned for the
Grail when Joseph separated the good from the evil. Now I wish
you to know that there have been two kings in Britain who have
been priests and emperors of Rome. And also I wish that you should
know that in Britain there will be a third king who will be priest and
emperor . . . But before you can be so noble and so valiant it is
necessary that the Round Table should be exalted again by you . . .
   'It happened formally that the Grail was given to Joseph when he
was in prison where Our Lord himself bore it to him. And when he
had come from the prison this Joseph entered into a wilderness and
many of the people of Judea with him . . .
   'Now, in truth, Our Lord made the first table, and Joseph made
the second, and I, in the time of Uther Pendragon, your father, had
the third made, which still will be much exalted . . . So know that
the Grail was given into the hands of Joseph, and upon his death he
left it to his brother-in-law who had the name of Bron. And this
Bron had twelve sons, one of whom was named Alain li Gros. And
the Fisher King commanded him to be the guardian of his brothers.
This Alain has come to this land from Judea, just as Our Lord has
commanded him . . .'

Merlin goes on to say that, having lived since the time of Christ, Bron the
Fisher King is now ill and will remain sick, unable to die, until a noble
knight of the Round Table travels to his castle and asks:

'What it is that the Grail has served and what it is it serves, then
immediately will the Fisher King be cured. And then he will tell

him the secret words of Our Lord and he will pass from life to death, and this knight will have the keeping of the blood of Jesus . . .'

Perceval, as Bron's grandson, is chosen to embark on the quest to cure the Fisher King. However, no one, including Perceval himself, knows where Bron's castle is. After many adventures Perceval eventually discovers the castle and is made welcome by his grandfather. As in the previous romances, a banquet follows.

Just as they seated themselves and the first course was brought to them, they saw come from a chamber a damsel very richly dressed who had a towel about her neck and bore in her hands two little silver platters. And after her came a youth who bore a lance, and it bled three drops of blood from its head; and they entered into a chamber before Perceval. And after this there came a youth and he bore between his hands the vessel that Our Lord gave to Joseph in the prison, and he bore it very high between his hands. And when the king saw it he bowed before it saying his *mea culpa* and all the others of the household did the same. When Perceval saw this he marvelled much and he might willingly have asked concerning it if he had not feared to annoy his host.

Perceval fails to ask about the Grail and, exhausted after his journey, falls asleep, awaking to discover the castle empty. On leaving the castle, he meets a damsel who tells him:

'You have been in the house of the rich Fisher King your grandfather and have seen pass before you the vessel in which is the blood of Our Lord – that which is called the Grail – and you have seen it pass before you three times, but you never enquired about it . . .'

As in Chrétien's story, Perceval cannot rediscover the Grail castle until he has proved himself a worthy knight. In this tale, however, he eventually succeeds. Not only does Perceval inherit the Grail, he is also told 'the secret words which Joseph taught', presumably the same secret words of Jesus referred to by Merlin in the opening passage of the story. Within a few years of the appearance of the *Didcot Perceval* in

France, Germany saw the first of its versions of the Grail romance, Wolfram von Eschenbach's *Parzival.*

[Wolfram's *Parzival*]

The Arthurian story found its way into Germany some time around 1200 in the form of two poems, *Erec* and *Iwein*, by the poet Hartmann von Aue. A year or so later, around 1205, the influential German poet Wolfram von Eschenbach composed his epic Grail romance *Parzival*, later to be immortalised in Wagner's opera *Parsifal.* It is essentially a reworking of Chrétien's *Le Conte del Graal*, although Wolfram provides many details absent from Chrétien's unfinished work. However, in *Parzival* the Grail is not a platter, a chalice, or even a head, but a magical stone called the Lapsit Excillis, from the Latin *lapis exilis*, meaning literally a small stone. According to Wolfram, it was with this stone that God had banished the angels who failed to support him in his battle with Lucifer.

In *Parzival*, the stone is in the keeping of a noble family who are entrusted with its protection. In return, they live in splendour on the food and drink that it miraculously provides. Additionally, the stone has the power to heal and preserve the life of its guardians. Contained within the walls of an impregnable castle, the Grail is protected by an order of knights, chosen as children when their names appear on the stone itself.

The story opens with Anfortas, king of the Grail castle, being mortally wounded, although the Grail's protection means that he cannot die. His only hope of freedom from the pain of his living death is if he can find a man to replace him. A message than appears on the stone telling the king that his heir, the son of his sister Herzelyde, will soon come to the castle. But only if the heir poses the right question will he prove himself worthy of succession.

Anfortas' nephew, and heir apparent, is none other than Parzival (the German rendering of Perceval), although he has been raised unaware of his true lineage. When he arrives at the castle he witnesses the same procession as Perceval in Chrétien's story, although the Grail is now the stone. After failing to ask the correct question, Parzival leaves and spends the remainder of the story acquiring wisdom by enlisting as one of Arthur's knights. Finally, he returns to the Grail castle and proves himself worthy of succession.

Beside the Grail being a stone, there are a number of other differences between Wolfram's story and those of his predecessors. For example, the Grail guardian is called Anfortas rather than Bron, and the warriors who protect the castle are not Arthurian characters but the Knights Templar. Where did the story originate? Fortunately Wolfram reveals his source. In his epilogue he refers to Chrétien's *Le Conte del Graal*, informing his readers that in it Chrétien had failed to do justice to a tale that already existed. He goes on to say that his own full and accurate portrayal of the original legend came from an Arabic manuscript discovered by his friend Kyot in Toledo, Spain.

If Wolfram is to be believed, then the original Grail legend appears to have been an Arabian story, probably adapted by the crusaders for a European readership. Many such poems were composed during the crusades by the visiting soldiers, who took Arabian tales and transformed them, with medieval heroes replacing the original Arab characters. However, in this assertion, Wolfram stands alone amongst the medieval Grail romancers.

[*Perlesvaus*]

Perlesvaus is another early Old French Grail romance, its title meaning 'the disinherited Perceval'. The anonymous author says that he translated the story from a Latin work in a 'holy house situated in the isle of Avalon, at the head of the Adventurous Marshes'; where this might be he does not explain. Regardless of his claim, the tale is very similar to the *Didcot Perceval* and probably comes from the same source.

The story opens with Gawain meeting a hermit who appears many years younger than he really is because he has 'long served in the Chapel of the Grail where the Grail is kept'. Guided by the hermit, Gawain discovers the Grail castle and is welcomed by the Fisher King and made guest of honour at a feast. To see the Grail, however, Gawain must prove himself worthy by retrieving a sword from the pagan king Gurgaran which had been used to decapitate John the Baptist. When he arrives at Gurgaran's castle Gurgaran tells Gawain that he will relinquish the sword only if the knight rescues his son from a giant. Ultimately, the giant is killed while distracted during a game of chess; his head is cut off and Gawain returns with it to Gurgaran. The sword is then returned to the Grail castle and placed with a number of other holy relics in the Grail chapel. Gawain then sees the Grail itself:

Lo, two damsels issued from a chapel, and one held in her hands the most holy Grail, and the other the lance of which the point bled into it . . . So sweet and so holy an odour accompanied the relics that they forgot to eat. Sir Gawain gazed at the Grail and it seemed to him that there was a chalice within it, albeit there was none at the time.

The second time the Grail appears Gawain sees a different vision within it:

Lo, the two damsels issued from the chapel and came again before Gawain, and he seemed to behold three angels where before he had beheld but two, and he seemed to behold in the midst of the Grail the form of a child.

It is brought in for a final time, and again Gawain experiences a vision:

Lo, the damsels came again before the table, and it seemed to Sir Gawain that there were three . . . He looked up and there appeared aloft a man nailed to a cross, and a spear was fixed in his side.

Having failed to ask the right questions about the Grail, Gawain fails in his quest and Perceval takes up the challenge, having to prove his worth by slaying the worshippers of a golden bull. Ultimately, with the help of the magic of his uncle Pelles, Perceval enters the castle and sees the Grail in the chapel, where it is kept along with the sword that Gawain recovered, a bell cast by Solomon, 'and other relics in great plenty'.

In the chapel Perceval hears a voice telling him that the relics must now be distributed amongst the monks of monasteries and churches in the surrounding area. It is also declared that:

'The Holy Grail shall appear here no longer, but within a short time you will know well where it will be.'

Finally Perceval sails away to a mysterious island, leaving Joseph, the son of King Pelles, to rule at the castle in his stead. We are not told where the Grail castle is, only that it is somewhere in Wales, as two Welsh knights many years later discover its ruins.

The Search for the Grail

[The Vulgate Cycle]

Coming from the Latin word *vulgare*, meaning to make public or translate in a popular fashion, the Vulgate Cycle contains two anonymous Grail romances, *Lancelot* and the *Queste del Saint Graal*, composed around 1220.

Lancelot recounts how five of Arthur's knights fail in their Grail quest, while the *Queste* has Perceval ultimately succeeding. Much within the stories is taken directly from the others so far discussed. However, two additional themes are of particular interest. Firstly, regarding the setting of the story, the Grail castle is described as being near *Le Velle Marche* – 'the Old Border'. Secondly, as in the First Continuation, there are seemingly two Grails involved. In the prefatory introduction to *Lancelot* we are told:

> On the eve of Good Friday . . . Arthur lay in his hut in one of the wildest regions of White Britain, plagued by doubts about the Trinity. Then Christ appeared to him and gave him a small book, no bigger than the palm of his hand, which would resolve all his doubts. He, Christ, had written it himself and only he who was purified by confession and fasting might read it. On the following morning he opened the book, the sections of which were scribed as follows: This is the book of thy descent. Here begins the book of the Holy Grail.

Here the Grail is clearly described as a book – a book written by Christ himself. However, later in the same story, it is described differently:

> It was made in the semblance of a chalice . . . Sir Gawain looked on the vessel, and esteemed it highly in his heart, yet knew not of what it was wrought; for it was not of wood nor of any manner of metal; nor was it in any wise of stone, nor of horn, nor of bone . . . Then he looked upon the maiden, and marvelled more at her beauty than at the wonder of the vessel.

With the Vulgate Cycle we come to the last of the important original Grail romances. One or two others did appear before the end of the third decade of the thirteenth century, such as those by the French poets Gerbert and Maessier; however, they add nothing to the story in the way of themes. Although scores of other Grail romances were to follow, culminating in Thomas Malory's famous version in his *Le Morte D'Arthur*, they were essentially rewrites of these original eight stories. None of the later authors claimed convincingly to have consulted some external, earlier surviving documentation as did the composers of the first romances. Yet even these earliest surviving tales may not have been the original medieval popularisations of the Grail story, as they were all written by continental authors, mainly in France, although their setting is always Britain and they involve British legendary heroes. It is probable therefore that the story was initially taken from some native British romance. In other words, there probably existed at least one, now lost, Grail romance upon which they were all based. So where did the story truly originate?

Summary

- The original Grail romances were some eight stories written within a period of about thirty years between 1190 and 1220: *Le Conte del Graal* by the French Chretien de Troyes, *circa* 1190; two anonymous Continuations of Chretien's story, *circa* 1195; Robert de Boron's *Joseph d'Arimathie* and the *Didcot Perceval*, *circa* 1200; *Parzival* by the German Wolfram von Eschenbach, *circa* 1205; and *Perlesvaus* and two stories in the Vulgate Cycle, *circa* 1220.

- *Le Conte del Graal* was the last of Chretien's five Arthurian romances, which was left unfinished when he died. The author neglects to describe the artefact's appearance, merely saying that it is made of gold and decorated with precious stones. The author of the First Continuation of Chretien's work also fails to explain what the Grail is, saying merely that it hovers around serving food. In the same story there is a second object also described as a Grail – a stone head carved in the likeness of Jesus.

- Although the First Continuation does not describe the Grail, it says that it had once belonged to Joseph of Arimathea, a theme incorporated by Robert de Boron within a year or two. In his *Joseph d'Arimathie*, however, Robert gives specific details about the Grail's appearance and origin, claiming that it was the cup used by Christ at the Last Supper, which Joseph obtained from Pilate after the Crucifixion.

• According to the anonymous author of the *Didcot Perceval* the story was originally written by a monk called Blayse. Again the Grail is the cup of the Last Supper. It is eventually brought to Britain – to the White Castle in the White Land – where it is guarded by Joseph's descendants. *Perlesvaus*, written a few years later, is so similar to the *Didcot Perceval* that it probably came from the same source. In this romance the Grail is not described, we are merely told that visions are seen within it.

• In Wolfram's *Parzival* the Grail is not a platter, a chalice, or even a head, but a magical stone called the Lapsit Excillis, from the Latin *lapsis exilis*, meaning literally a small stone. The Vulgate Cycle adds another Grail to the story: like the First Continuation, there are two Grails, one the chalice of the Last Supper and the other a book written by Jesus himself.

• Although all these romances were written by continental authors, mainly in France, the setting is always Britain and they involve British legendary heroes. It is likely therefore that the story was taken from some original British legend. Accordingly, there may have existed at least one, now lost, Grail romance upon which they were all based.

Chapter V

The Apostolic Heresy

We know that by the late twelfth century the Grail story was widely disseminated, as the romance authors name a variety of different sources discovered all across Europe, from the Swiss Alps to southern Spain. This means that the legend must have been in existence for some considerable time before the surviving romances were compiled. What *was* the original legend upon which the Grail romances were based?

Firstly, we need to ascertain exactly what the Grail really was. In Wolfram's *Parzival* it is a magical stone. As we have seen, this was almost certainly based on an Arabian legend, and so seemingly had no connection with Christian tradition. Other crusader tales of similar sacred stones appeared throughout Christendom during the crusades. However, even though the other contemporary romances concerned Christian relics, like Wolfram's story the Grail itself is often something other than the cup of Christ.

In *Le Conte del Graal* it is far from clear what Chrétien's Grail actually is. Obviously it is some form of holy relic associated with the mass, as the Rich Fisher is sustained by a mass wafer served from it. This has prompted speculation that the Grail was originally some form of dish or platter, as a mass wafer is unlikely to have been served from a cup. Additionally, Chretien gives the impression that *graals* were relatively common objects in his day, for he simply refers to it as *un graal*, 'a graal', and not *le Graal*, 'the Graal', as Robert de Boron later does. In fact, Robert de Boron goes on to describe it in even more venerating terms as *Le Saint Grail*, 'The Holy Grail'.

Chretien's lack of detail implies that *graal* was a word familiar to his contemporary readership, although the meaning has since fallen from use. It has been suggested that the word could be derived from *gradale*. A number of medieval French inventories of household possessions refer

43

to items under this name, which possibly comes from the Latin *gradus* meaning 'in stages', and probably applied to a dish or platter that was brought to the table at various stages during a meal.

Whatever the word originally meant, it was quite clear, even from a cursory examination of the romances, that the Grail was different things to different writers. Chrétien's Grail could have been the plate used by Christ at the Last Supper; the First Continuation has two Grails, one seemingly a floating dish and the other a carved head of Jesus; Robert and the *Didcot* author have it as the cup of the Last Supper; the *Perlesvaus* Grail seems to be a nebulous artefact in which visions associated with Christ's life appear; and the Vulgate version has the Grail as both a chalice and a holy book.

Apart from Wolfram's stone, which clearly came from a completely separate tradition, all these Grails seem to be holy relics associated with Jesus. Whatever it originally meant, around the year 1200 the word Grail seems to have become a collective word for holy relics associated with Christ himself, as opposed to the ordinary relics of mere saints. Indeed, in all the early romances the Grail is kept together with other holy relics; seemingly the most holy of relics, as they are each directly associated with the Bible, such as the sword that beheaded John the Baptist, the lance that pierced Christ's side, and the bell made by Solomon. *Perlesvaus* actually describes a chapel specifically built to house these relics, which the author collectively calls 'the Grail Hallows'. By the late thirteenth century, however, the word Grail applied almost exclusively to the cup of the Last Supper.

Something the original romances do have in common is that they all set their story in Britain, each associating the Grail with King Arthur and his knights. Is there therefore anything in early Welsh poetry, which existed before the romances, to couple Arthur with such a relic? Although neither the Holy Grail nor any other Jesus relic appears in the surviving Welsh Arthurian stories, there are similar tales of Arthur searching for a magical cauldron. Two early Welsh tales, *Culhwch and Olwen* and *The Spoils of Annwn*, both include Arthur and his warriors searching for a cauldron which, like the Grail, has supernatural, life-preserving properties. As the quest for the cauldron is so similar to the later Grail quests, were the Grail romances influenced by these Celtic legends? Was the Grail originally a cauldron having no association with Christ or the Last Supper?

The Spoils of Annwn is now preserved in *The Book of Taliesin* (in the

National Library of Wales, Aberystwyth), a manuscript dating from around 1300. On linguistic analysis most scholars date the original poem to around 900. In it we read of Arthur's theft of the cauldron from the island of Annwn. It could have been from this poem that the legends of both the Grail and the isle of Avalon originated, perhaps as attempts to medievalise Celtic mythology. The similarities with the Grail and Avalon legends cannot be ignored, particularly when Annwn is depicted as a land which lies across the water – a mystical island containing the magical cauldron. In the romances Avalon is often depicted as the island where the Grail is hidden. Indeed, the link between Annwn and Avalon is further substantiated when we see that in *The Spoils of Annwn* a citadel on the island is called the 'fort of glass', the same name used by Geoffrey of Monmouth to describe Avalon's castle.

Similar links exist in the tale of *Culhwch and Olwen*, now preserved in *The Red Book of Hergest*, a Welsh manuscript in the Bodleian Library compiled around 1400. Again from linguistic analysis the poem appears to date from the tenth century. In it, the hero, Culhwch, bids for the hand in marriage of Olwen, the daughter of the giant Ysbaddaden. However, the giant, intent on preventing their marriage, imposes a series of impossible tasks on Culhwch which he must complete if he is to win his bride. On the advice of his father, the hero travels to the court of Arthur and acquires his assistance. For much of the story it is Arthur himself who leads the quest on Culhwch's behalf: he rescues the god-king Mabon, hunts down a giant boar, and attacks Ireland to carry off the magical cauldron. There are clearly parallels between the tale of *Culhwch and Olwen* and *The Spoils of Annwn*. The attack on Ireland to seize the cauldron is reminiscent of the raid on the isle of Annwn, and in both tales Arthur's ship is called *Prydwen*.

In *The Spoils of Annwn* the cauldron is guarded by nine virgin priestesses, similar to the nine Grail maidens in the Vulgate romances. The idea of nine saintly women living in seclusion could certainly have been of very early Celtic origin. The first-century classical geographer Pomponius Mela, for instance, writes of nine priestesses living under a vow of chastity on an island off the coast of Brittany. These women were of a Celtic tribe similar to the Britons themselves, and were said to have the power to heal the sick and foretell the future.

There are many examples of magical cauldrons in Celtic literature, such as the cauldron of the legendary King Dagda in Irish folklore.

Indeed, in the tale of *Culhwch and Olwen* it is to Ireland that Arthur goes in search of the cauldron. Moreover, in this story the cauldron is said to belong to King Di-wrnach, very possibly a Welsh rendering of the Irish Dagda.

It therefore seems fairly certain that at least some aspects of the Grail story were taken from these Welsh Arthurian tales. Historically, cauldrons believed to contain magical properties were treasured by Celtic chieftains, as described by Julius Caesar in the first century BC. It can be argued that they were a pre-Christian equivalent of holy relics. Many Celtic traditions continued side by side with Christianity, so such a cauldron could have been associated with the historical Arthur of the fifth century. Significantly, a sacred cauldron has even been found at the site suggested by our research as the burial place of Owain Ddantgwyn – the warrior we believe to have been the historical Arthur.

The Dark Age poem *The Song of Llywarch the Old* not only calls the Powysian kings the heirs of Arthur, it also names the burial site of the dynasty. In one of the monologue passages in the saga, *The Song of Heledd*, Cynddylan, the king of Powys in the 650s, is mourned by his sister Heledd. She relates how his body is taken for burial to *Eglwyseu Bassa*, the Churches of Bassa. From the poem, it is clear that the Churches of Bassa had long been the family burial ground, for Heledd also refers to 'the gravemound of Gorwynnion' and other 'green graves' at the site. In a second elegy on Cynddylan's death within the poem, another of his family, Llywarch, says that he will 'grieve for the death of Cynddlyan' until he too 'rests beneath the mound'. *The Song of Llywarch the Old* firmly identifies the long-lost burial site of the Dark Age Powysian kings. As Owain Ddantgwyn was one such king, the Churches of Bassa could well have been his last resting place.

The Churches of Bassa is almost certainly the village today called Baschurch, some nine miles to the north-west of Shrewsbury. In secluded countryside on the edge of the village is the Berth, an ancient fortified hillock surrounded by marshland and linked to the mainland by a gravel causeway. The hill is completely encompassed by Iron Age earth and stone ramparts, and joined to a low-lying oval enclosure by a second causeway some 150 metres to the north-east.

The Berth, whose name is thought to derive from the Saxon word *burh*, meaning castle or fort, but more likely comes from the old Welsh word *berth* meaning sanctified or sacred, was certainly in use during the sixth century, since archaeological excavations in 1962–3 uncovered fragments of pottery dating from the period. As *The Song of Heledd* specifically refers to the king's graves being in Travail's Acre, the precise burial site is probably what is now called the Sacred Enclosure, an area of about an acre, surrounded by Iron Age earthworks, 150 metres to the north of the Berth itself. The Sacred Enclosure has never been excavated, so the remains of Cynddylan, his ancestors, and the historical Arthur may still lie there silently awaiting discovery.

An isolated site, silent and eerie, the last resting place of the man who was Arthur could hardly be more appropriate. In the past, after heavy rain, the marshy area surrounding the hill would have become a shallow mere. Centuries ago, therefore, the Berth could have appeared almost as an island rising above the waterlogged terrain. (More recently the area has been drained to form arable farmland.) In other words, it was once an island, perhaps the original Avalon or Annwn of legend.

Interestingly, it was at the Berth that an early Celtic cauldron was found – one which seems to have been an ancient religious artefact. In 1906 a workman cutting turf discovered a bronze cauldron, some forty-five centimetres high and thirty centimetres wide, which was presented to the British Museum, where it was dated from the early first century. Archaeologists concluded that it had originally been cast into the waters surrounding the Berth as a votive offering to an ancient water spirit. It was therefore no ordinary cooking vessel, but a sacred cauldron such as that for which Arthur searches in the early Welsh tales. Although it was made in the first century, the precise date that the cauldron was cast into the water has been impossible to determine. It may therefore have been in the possession of some important Powysian chieftain – perhaps the historical Arthur – as late as the fifth century.

These Celtic cauldron legends almost certainly influenced the development of the medieval Grail legend. As each successive romancer chose to embellish his story, relevant themes in early Welsh literature were probably adapted and medievalised for the purpose. However, Celtic mythology and Welsh cauldron legends only played a limited part in influencing the Grail tradition of the Middle Ages. The most important themes within all the early romances are purely Christian in concept.

In each romance the Grail or Grails are kept by the family of Perceval, the direct descendants of Joseph of Arimathea. The authors go to considerable lengths to explain this lineage and its significance – Joseph is appointed as Grail guardian by Christ himself. Here lies the Grail's importance – it is a visible, tangible symbol of an alternative apostolic succession.

According to Catholic doctrine, the Pope is the direct spiritual successor of the apostle St Peter who, according to the Bible, was appointed by Jesus as head of the Church. No one other than Peter's successor and his ordained priests can perform mass or hear confession. Called the apostolic succession, this idea is central to Catholic faith. Without the mass and confession there can be no salvation, hence the Catholic Church retains absolute spiritual authority.

In the Grail romances, however, we read that it is not Peter, but Joseph of Arimathea who is given the cup Christ used to perform the Last Supper – the very first mass. To the Church authorities of the Middle Ages, such a notion would be pure heresy. Surely if the cup had been given to anyone it would have been given to St Peter, and would still be in the hands of the popes. We are left in little doubt that this is the primary theme of the romances, as in the *Didcot* and Vulgate versions of the story Christ instructs Joseph in 'the secret words of Jesus'. Moreover, in *Perlesvaus* he is even taught the mysteries of the mass – something which according to the Church was strictly reserved for Catholic priests ordained through the apostolic succession from St Peter.

What the Grail romances are clearly implying is that there supposedly existed an alternative apostolic line of succession through Joseph of Arimathea and his family. Moreover, this line is claimed to have secret knowledge, unknown to the established Church. The Vulgate romances go so far as to make one of their Grails a book written by Jesus himself – something that no Catholic relic-hunter ever dared boast to have found. Most indicative of all is the hereditary name for the Grail guardian, the Rich Fisher or Fisher King. In the Bible Peter was a fisherman. Indeed, the papal legacy was, and still is, referred to as the 'shoes of the fisherman', meaning that, once appointed, the Pope, Christ's representative on Earth, has taken over the role originally given to Peter by Jesus himself. The Fisher King is seemingly, therefore, nothing less than an alternative pope.

This central theme of the romances seems to have been overlooked by the Church authorities at the time, otherwise the Inquisition of 1223, established by Pope Gregory IX to root out heresy, would have come crashing down on offenders. The romancers were lucky. All the same, for them to have risked papal wrath at a time when the Roman Catholic Church was at the height of its political power implies that there was more at stake than art for its own sake. Before we can begin to investigate what this might have been, we must first determine if there is any truth to the story of Joseph of Arimathea. Equally, is there historical evidence that the cup of Christ survived to become a Christian relic?

All four gospels tell how, after the Crucifixion, the rich disciple Joseph of Arimathea obtained Jesus' body from Pilate, wrapped it in a linen cloth and laid it in the tomb. St John's Gospel adds that another convert, Nicodemus, helped with the burial:

> And after this Joseph of Arimathea, being a disciple of Jesus, but secretly for fear of the Jews, besought Pilate that he might take away the body of Jesus: and Pilate gave him leave. He came therefore and took the body of Jesus. And there came also Nicodemus, which at the first came to Jesus by night, and brought a mixture of myrrh and aloes, about an hundred pound weight. Then took they the body of Jesus, and wound it in linen clothes with the spices, as the manner of the Jews is to bury.

This is virtually all the Bible tells us of Joseph and Nicodemus. There is nothing concerning their backgrounds, what became of them, nor any reference to Joseph in connection with the cup of the Last Supper. As we have seen, Nicodemus also appears in the Grail romances, and an early document, supposedly concerning his life as a Christian, proves that much of the Joseph story outlined in the Grail romances existed at least as early as the fourth century.

In the fourth-century *Evangelium Nicodemi*, now in the Vatican, we read that at the trial before Pilate, Nicodemus testified in Jesus' defence and became a converted follower. The manuscript is supposedly written by Nicodemus himself, and concerns the struggle of the early Christians in Jerusalem. Much of the opening section relates to Joseph of Arimathea, describing how, after he had deposited Jesus' body in the tomb, the Jews imprisoned him. However, on Easter Day Christ appeared to Joseph and set him free, after which he travelled to preach the word.

The *Evangelium Nicodemi* certainly shows that early Christians in the pre-Catholic empire considered Joseph of Arimathea to be one of the first leaders of Christ's Church. However, it does not show that any of them considered him to be *the* leader, neither does it mention the cup of the Last Supper. However, a second manuscript dating from the same period, the *Vindicta Salvatoris* (also in the Vatican), says that Joseph set out to found a Church in the far north, after the Roman plundering of Jerusalem in AD 70. In fact, this is exactly what we read in Robert de Boron's *Joseph d'Arimathie*. Although neither the *Evangelium Nicodemi* nor the *Vindicta Salvatoris* includes the cup of Christ, they do show that, in outline, the story of Joseph recounted in the medieval Grail romances was being told over eight centuries earlier.

Did Joseph of Arimathea really found a Church in Britain? It is recorded in the mid fifth century that an alternative Church still survived in Britain – just prior to the historical Arthurian era. Called Pelagianism, was this the Church of Joseph?

Pelagianism takes its name from the priest Pelagius, a Briton who preached a doctrine in opposition to the established Church. Where his ideas originated is unknown, but sometime around 380 he left Britain for Rome, where he came into conflict with the Pope. Although he disagreed with the establishment on a number of issues, it was his teachings throwing the apostolic succession into doubt that aroused the greatest anger. Although there is no direct evidence to link Pelagius with a Church founded by Joseph of Arimathea, he did question whether the true apostolic succession originated with St Peter. In 416, the Church responded by proclaiming his teachings a heresy. Not only the Church but the State itself stood to suffer if such dangerous ideas took hold, as they did for a while in Britain and Gaul. At this time Catholic Christianity was virtually all that was holding the empire together. Therefore, in 425 Emperor Honorius was persuaded by the Pope to issue an imperial command to the Pelagian bishops of Gaul. They must renounce their heresy before the Bishop of Arles within twenty days, or face the severest consequences.

Although the policy was successful elsewhere, the problem remained in Britain, over which Honorius had no direct control. St Germanus, the rich and powerful Bishop of Auxerre, was thus dispatched to Britain as a missionary to combat the Pelagian heresy. The contemporary writer Prosper of Aquitaine, who dedicated himself to attacking Pelagianism, wrote of the year 429:

The Pelagian Agricola, son of the Pelagian bishop Severianus, corrupts the churches of Britain by insinuating his doctrine. But at the suggestion of the deacon Palladius, Pope Celestine sends Germanus bishop of Auxerre as his representative, and after the confusion of the heretics guides the Britons to the Catholic faith.

Little is known about the beliefs of the Pelagians, beyond their questioning of the apostolic succession of St Peter, but it is possible that Pelagius, Agricola, Severianus, and their followers were subscribing to a doctrine believed to have originated with Joseph of Arimathea. According to the *Vindicta Salvatoris* Joseph founded a Church in the far north of the empire; since Britain was the empire's northernmost province, it is possible that it was centred here.

Remarkably, Pelagianism may not only be linked with the Joseph of Arimathea story as it appears in the Grail romances, but also with the historical King Arthur.

In his *Historia Brittonum* Nennius relates how the British chieftain Vortigern came into conflict with Germanus shortly after he arrived in Britain to combat Pelagianism. According to Nennius, Germanus 'preached at Vortigern, to convert him to his Lord'. It seems, therefore, that Vortigern was himself a Pelagian. According to Germanus' biographer, Constantius of Lyon, the bishop's deputation to Britain was received in St Albans by a delegation of clergy from the city, who were soon reconverted to orthodox Catholicism. With the success of St Albans under his belt, Germanus moved on to preach across the country, converting not only the laity but also the troops, who chose to turn against the heresy of their leader. This again seemingly refers to the chief British warlord Vortigern.

According to Constantius, Germanus confronted Vortigern at the very heart of Pelagian heresy – his capital city. Constantius neglects to name the city, but since Bede, Gildas, Nennius and the *Anglo-Saxon Chronicle* all record that Vortigern ruled most of Britain shortly after the Romans left, it must have been the most important city of the time. As we have seen from both the historical and the archaeological evidence, Viroconium was the principal city of early-fifth-century Britain, and therefore was almost certainly the religious centre for Pelagianism. Again, we return full circle to Viroconium and the historical Arthur:

• The Grail romances concern an alternative apostolic succession centred on Britain.

51

- Pelagianism claimed an alternative apostolic succession and was centred on the British capital Viroconium.

- Viroconium seems to have been the capital of the historical Arthur.

- King Arthur and his knights are the central characters in all the Grail romances.

Perhaps Arthur was included in the Grail romances not simply to popularise the story, as previously thought, but because he was *genuinely* associated with historical events from which the Grail legend evolved.

Summary

- According to Catholic doctrine, the Pope is the direct spiritual successor of the apostle St Peter who, according to the Bible, was appointed by Jesus as head of the Church. No one other than Peter's successor and his ordained priests can perform mass or hear confession. Called the apostolic succession, this idea is central to Catholic faith. Without the mass and confession there can be no salvation, hence the Catholic Church retains absolute spiritual authority.

- In the Grail romances we read that it is not St Peter but Joseph of Arimathea who is given the cup Christ used to perform the Last Supper – the very first mass. In the *Didcot* the Vulgate versions of the story Christ instructs Joseph in 'the secret words of Jesus', and in *Perlesvaus* Joseph is even taught the mysteries of the mass – something which according to the Church was strictly reserved for Catholic priests ordained through the apostolic succession from St Peter. What the Grail romances are implying is that there existed an alternative apostolic line of succession through Joseph of Arimathea and his descendants.

- Most indicative of all is the hereditary name for the Grail guardian, the Rich Fisher or Fisher King. In the Bible Peter, the first pope, was a fisherman. Indeed, the papal legacy was, and still is, referred to as the 'shoes of the fisherman'. The Fisher King seems, therefore, to be nothing less than an alternative pope.

• From Vatican records we know that during the early fifth century the Church in Britain was preaching an alternative apostolic succession. Known as Pelagianism (after one of its exponents, Pelagius), it dared to question the authority of the Roman popes. Although most records of their doctrine were destroyed, it is possible that the Pelagians believed that their succession descended from Joseph of Arimathea. Two fourth-century documents in the Vatican, the *Evangelium Nicodemi* and the *Vindicta Salvatoris*, demonstrate that early Christians in the pre-Catholic empire considered Joseph of Arimathea to be the first leader of Christ's Church. The *Vindicta Salvatoris* even suggests that Joseph was believed to have founded his Church in Britain.

• According to the fifth-century writer Prosper of Aquitaine, in 429 the Pope sent Germanus, the Bishop of Auxerre, to Britain to combat Pelagianism. The heresy seems to have been centred on the city of Viroconium, as according to Germanus' biographer, Constantius, the bishop confronted Vortigern at his capital. Bede, Gildas, Nennius and the *Anglo-Saxon Chronicle* all record that Vortigern held sway over all the Britons during this time, and both the historical and the archaeological evidence indicates that Viroconium was the most important city in fifth-century Britain.

• The Grail romances concern a purported alternative apostolic succession centred on Britain; Pelagianism claimed an alternative apostolic succession and seems to have been centred on Viroconium; Viroconium appears to have been the capital of the historical Arthur; and King Arthur and his knights are the central characters in all the Grail romances. The Grail romances may therefore have evolved from legends derived from real events associated with the historical Arthur.

Chapter VI

The Treasure of the White Land

Pelagianism offers only circumstantial evidence to couple the Grail romances with the city from where Arthur is most likely to have ruled. However, the romances themselves provide a direct link between the setting for the Grail quest and the Dark Age city of Viroconium. During the Dark Ages Powys was called the White Land and Viroconium was known as the White Town; in the Grail romances the Grail castle is said to be in or near the White Town in the White Land.

In the First Continuation we are told how Joseph founds his Church in Britain, in somewhere known as the White Land. The *Didcot Perceval* has Perceval and Gawain involved in a contest near the Grail castle, the location described as 'the White Castle in the White Town'. In *Perlesvaus* a similar contest takes place in the 'White Hall of the White Town', while the Vulgate Grail romances both refer to the Grail castle being the 'White Castle' in 'The Old Border'.

In addition to the Grail romances there survives a Welsh story, written in the mid twelfth century, which seems to be based on Chrétien's *Le Conte del Graal*. Called *Peredur*, after its hero, it now survives in *The Red Book of Hergest* and appears to be a Welsh rendering of the Perceval tale. Peredur is invited to attend a banquet and witnesses a procession almost identical to that which Perceval sees in the Grail castle. In *Peredur*, however, the Grail is replaced by a head on a silver platter. In this particular story the banquet is held in the 'White Hall', in the 'White Town', in the 'White Land'. In Geoffrey of Monmouth's 1135 *History of the Kings of Britain*, Arthur's kingdom is called the White Land. Furthermore, many of the early Welsh tales which include King Arthur, such as *The Dialogue of Arthur* (*circa* 1150), refer to Arthur's court as the 'White Hall'. These last three references were made some years

54

before Chrétien de Troyes introduced the name Camelot in the late twelfth century.

Although these references fail to provide a geographical location for the White Land and the White Town, they must have been respectively the kingdom of Powys and the Roman city of Viroconium. By the seventh century native Britons referred to Powys as the White Land and to Viroconium as the White Town. This is known from the Dark Age war poem *The Song of Llywarch the Old*, considered to be an accurate account of events in seventh-century Powys. The poem refers to the Saxon invasion of the kingdom in 658 as 'the plunder of the White Land' and the sacking of its capital as 'the burning of the White Town'. The name White Town probably originated from the time of the late Roman occupation, when the legion garrisoned at Viroconium was known as the White Legion. This legion is recorded in the *Notitia Dignitatum*, a Roman register of imperial officers compiled around 420. It seems that after the Romans departed, the rulers of Powys referred to their kingdom as the White Land and their capital as the White Town to emphasise their claimed succession from the former imperial governors.

The Song of Llywarch the Old also describes the royal palace in the town as 'the White Hall of Powys'. The White Hall, in the White Town, in the White Land – these are precisely the words often used in the Grail romances to describe the Grail castle and its locality.

From the archaeological evidence we know for certain that the White Hall of Powys historically existed. The latest excavations at Viroconium have shown that the city did have a splendid winged mansion at its heart, destroyed by the Saxons some time in the mid seventh century. There can be little doubt that *The Song of Llywarch the Old* is referring to this particular mansion as the White Hall, since the poet describes one of his characters gazing down at the ruins from Wrekin Hill, which directly overlooks the site. Moreover, archaeologists have dated pottery from the period of the mansion's destruction to the mid seventh century, and the poem refers to the burning of the White Hall during the Saxon invasion of the kingdom in 658. (This date is known from both the tenth-century *Welsh Annals* and the ninth-century *Anglo-Saxon Chronicle*.)

The Grail story seems, therefore, to have been set in the kingdom of Powys. Both the historical evidence and the earliest legends locate King Arthur in Powys. Nearly all the Grail romances make specific reference to the White Land, White Town, White Castle or White Hall. In the Arthurian period, the White Town was the capital of Powys –

Viroconium – where it is known from *The Song of Llywarch the Old* and from archaeology that there stood an historical White Hall. At the very least this suggests that the Grail romancers were basing their stories on much earlier tales which located Arthur in an historical setting. Remember, when the romances were written it was widely believed that Arthur came from Tintagel or Glastonbury. If the romancers were simply concocting their stories to please their readership, they would surely have set their scenes in the south of England – not in some mysterious White Town in a forgotten White Land.

Although there may be good reason to believe that the Joseph of Arimathea story was based to some degree on real events, and that a Church or sect thought to have been founded by him may have had genuine associations with the historical Arthur, there was still no direct evidence to couple either of them with an historical Grail. Indeed, there is no reference to the cup of Christ anywhere outside the Bible pre-dating the romances of the twelfth century. Maybe the Holy Grail was simply a medieval myth, after all, having no genuine associations with the historical Arthur or the original Joseph of Arimathea story. Perhaps the Celtic cauldron legends became the Holy Grail of Chrétien and the other French romancers.

However, the Grail romances concern Christian relics: the lance that pierced the side of Christ, the sword used to behead John the Baptist, a book written by Jesus himself, a bell made by Solomon, and Christ's head carved by Nicodemus, and indeed, the cup. There is nothing pagan about any of these; the central themes of the Grail romances are entirely Christian. Even though the association of the Grail with Avalon appears to have been taken from the pagan cauldron and Annwn legends, the story of the Holy Grail itself must have originated with Christian tradition.

Regardless of any authentic associations with Biblical times, were these relics historical artefacts thought to be the genuine items at the time the romances were compiled? One of the Grails certainly was – the carved head of Jesus described in the First Continuation historically existed at the time the romance was written. It was housed at Lucca Cathedral in Tuscany and attracted pilgrims from all over Europe. Called the *Volto Santo*, it was believed to be the only true likeness of Jesus ever made, by either sculptor or painter. As this Grail was based on a relic that historically existed, perhaps the others were too.

Did a genuine relic, thought to be the cup of Christ, really exist during the Middle Ages? If so, where? Nearly all the romances place the Holy Grail in the White Land, in or near the White Town. As the First Continuation had been absolutely right about where the *Volto Santo* was to be found, perhaps an historical chalice, considered to be the Holy Grail, similarly survived in the vicinity of Viroconium. One verse in *The Song of Llywarch the Old* describes a remarkably similar event to a scene in the *Perlesvaus* Grail romance. According to the former:

> Cynddlyan, vested in purple, divided the royal treasure. The abbots, vested in white, took each a holy relic. And all swore to protect them from heathen plunder.

In *Perlesvaus*, Perceval hears a voice telling him that the relics housed in the Grail chapel must be distributed amongst the monasteries and churches in the surrounding area. Could there be a connection?

The Song of Llywarch the Old gives no details concerning the nature of the relics or where they were taken. All we are told is that before the Saxons invaded, the Powysian king Cynddylan called a meeting of his clergy, handed over the relics, and ordered the abbots to preserve them. No contemporary records survive from pre-Saxon Powys, but a number of legends exist in Shropshire folklore which talk of the lost treasures of Powys, hidden when the Saxons invaded in the seventh century. This is the precise period to which *The Song of Llywarch the Old* refers.

The Cynddylan named in the poem was an actual historical figure, a direct descendant of Owain Ddantgwyn, the warrior we believe to have been the historical Arthur. He was the last Briton to rule Powys before most of the kingdom was conquered by the Saxon king Oswy in 658, and died attempting to defend the kingdom while his people fled into what are now the Welsh Marches. The survivors established a new kingdom in central Wales, but the fertile English Midlands remained in Saxon hands.

The Song of Llywarch the Old is considered to be an accurate account of the events surrounding the sacking of Powys. Both the leaders and the battles in the poem are recorded in contemporary Irish chronicles and in the tenth-century *Welsh Annals*, and are referenced in the ninth-century *Anglo-Saxon Chronicle*. Local landmarks and geographical features are accurately described, and the events in the poem are outlined in cold military terms, unfettered by myth of elaboration. There seems no reason to doubt, therefore, that the relics did exist, and were hidden as described.

Unfortunately, no subsequent record of these Powysian relics survives. However, they may be referenced in an earlier, classical text. As discussed in Chapter I, the medieval Grail romance could have arisen from legends concerning the Marian Chalice, the Christian relic taken from Rome when the city was sacked in AD 410. According to the fifth-century historian Olympiodorus, it was taken with other sacred artefacts to the isle of Britain, as the province was considered relatively safe from the full-scale barbarian invasions threatening the rest of the Western Empire. Indeed, Britain was about the *only* safe place to where the Emperor Honorius could dispatch the relics. In 410 the Western Empire was technically in a state of civil war with the Eastern Empire based at Constantinople, and consequently no sanctuary could be expected anywhere in the East.

There is no reason to doubt that the removal of the chalice to Britain was an historical event, as Olympiodorus is a primary, reliable source for historians studying the late Roman Empire. An Egyptian Greek, born around 365, he dealt in his twenty-two books with the years 407–25, and is considered by modern scholars to have been an accurate and objective chronicler of the contemporary events of his time. Indeed, very often his writing is supported by surviving records from Constantinople.

If the Marian Chalice and the other relics were brought to Britain as Olympiodorus states, then their most likely destination would have been the city of Viroconium. In AD 410 northern and eastern Britain were already suffering incursions by the Picts and Germanic raiders. The three most important cities, London, Lincoln and York, were repeatedly threatened, which left Viroconium as the most important Roman city during the final years of Roman occupation. As we have seen, the archaeological evidence shows that the city was rebuilt around AD 400, while the previously more important cities were being abandoned. Viroconium was the last Roman capital of Britain, and so the most likely destination for the relics.

Unfortunately, Olympiodorus fails to name the other relics. However, they must have included some important religious artefacts for their safety to have been considered so imperative. Two centuries later, when the city of Viroconium itself was finally sacked, its ruler Cynddylan ordered the hiding of what must have been similarly important relics. Were they one and the same?

No further record has ever surfaced concerning the fate of the Roman relics. Rome was eventually recaptured from the Visigoths, but it is possible that the artefacts remained in Britain. Within a few months of the relics leaving Rome, the last of the legions were withdrawn from Britain. Within a few years the Britons had establised an autonomous administration, so it is unlikely that they would have returned anything of great religious significance to Honorius. Although the Pope may have ordered the relics returned to Rome, it is equally unlikely that the British Church would have surrendered them. As we have seen, at the time the power of the Pope was being severely questioned in Britain.

Surely there must be a connection between the Marian Chalice and the Holy Grail:

• The Roman relics included the Marian Chalice which was believed to have held the blood of Christ.

• In the Grail romances the Holy Grail is a chalice which held the blood of Christ.

• The most likely destination of the Roman relics, including the Marian Chalice, was the British city of Viroconium.

• The medieval romances appear to have been set in Powys in the vicinity of Viroconium.

• The romance *Perlesvaus* refers to the Grail chapel relics being hidden in a similar fashion to *The Song of Llywarch the Old*'s description of the hiding of the relics of Powys.

If the Marian Chalice did inspire the theme of the Holy Grail as the cup of Christ, then the story of Joseph bringing the Grail to Britain would be inaccurate. The Marian Chalice was only discovered in AD 327 by the Empress Helena in the Holy Sepulchre in Jerusalem. Neither was it associated with Joseph of Arimathea, but with Mary Magdalene. There may, however, have been a confusion of two separate traditions. The *Evangelium Nicodemi* says that Joseph escaped from prison to begin his ministry immediately after the Resurrection, whereas the *Vindicta Salvatoris* says that he remained incarcerated until the fall of Jerusalem some forty years later. Exactly the same discrepancy is echoed in the

Grail romances, in which the First Continuation agrees with the *Vindicta Salvatoris*, while Robert de Boron's *Joseph d'Arimathie* tallies with the *Evangelium Nicodemi*. This shows that for at least eight centuries before the Grail romances were written there were conflicting accounts concerning Joseph's life. Perhaps there had been similar disagreement regarding the cup of the Last Supper.

It remains a mystery why Empress Helena should have thought that the cup found in the Holy Sepulchre had ever been used to collect the blood of Christ. However, she may have been influenced by surviving legends concerning the cup used by Joseph. St John's Gospel relates how Mary Magdalene had visited the Holy Sepulchre to find the tomb empty, and a late Grail romance written around 1225 by the French poet Gerbert de Montreuil (sometimes called the Fourth Continuation) says that Joseph had obtained the Grail from Mary on the day of the Resurrection. Perhaps such a legend already existed during the Empress Helena's time, a legend coupling the Grail with both Mary Magdalene and Joseph of Arimathea.

Although Gerbert's story adds little to the original eight Grail romances, it does address one important issue that the others neglect. Namely, how Joseph of Arimathea knew about the cup of the Last Supper in the first place. In the Biblical account he is not present at the Last Supper, neither is he previously named as a disciple of Jesus. For the Grail story to maintain its internal logic, it must be assumed that someone close to Jesus told Joseph of the cup's significance – presumably Mary Magdalene.

The Gerbert romance suggests that a legend could have survived that Joseph had obtained the cup from Mary. Perhaps it was thought that the cup remained in, or was later returned to the tomb by Joseph himself. Such a legend may have led Empress Helena to believe that the cup she found in the Holy Sepulchre had been used by Mary Magdalene to collect Christ's blood, while at the same time believing it to be the same vessel used at the Last Supper.

The Marian Chalice could well have sparked a legend which later inspired the medieval Grail romances. It is certainly the nearest historical equivalent to the Holy Grail yet discovered. There is a strong possibility it was once housed in the city of Viroconium, and the reliable *Song of Llywarch the Old* references a collection of relics being hidden somewhere in the area in 658. Unfortunately, even if these relics did include the Marian Chalice, the poem leaves no clues as to what became of them. However, if these were the Roman relics referenced by Olympiodorus, then they would presumably have been in Viroconium from around AD 410 to 658. The Marian Chalice may therefore have been in Viroconium at the same time that the city served as the capital for Owain Ddantgwyn. Accordingly, we must return to King Arthur's role in the Grail mystery.

Summary

- In the First Continuation we are told how Joseph founds his Church in Britain, in somewhere it calls the White Land. The *Didcot Perceval* has Perceval and Gawain involved in a contest near the Grail castle, the location described as 'the White Castle in the White Town'. In *Perlesvaus* a similar contest takes place in the 'White Hall of the White Town', while the Vulgate Grail romances both refer to the Grail castle being the 'White Castle'.

- By the seventh century the native Britons referred to Powys as the White Land and to Viroconium as the White Town. This is known from the Dark Age war poem *The Song of Llywarch the Old*, considered to be an accurate account of events in seventh-century Powys. The poem refers to the Saxon invasion of the kingdom in 658 as 'the plunder of the White Land' and the sacking of its capital as 'the burning of the White Town'.

- In the *Perlesvaus* romance Perceval hears a voice telling him that the relics housed in the Grail chapel must be distributed amongst the monasteries and churches in the surrounding area. *The Song of Llywarch the Old* says that before the Saxons invaded, the Powysian king Cynddylan called a meeting of his clergy, handed over to them a number of important relics, and ordered the abbots of Powys to preserve them. Could they be one and the same?

- Unfortunately, no subsequent record of these Powysian relics survives. However, they may be referenced in an earlier, classical text. The medieval Grail romance could have arisen from legends concerning the Marian Chalice, the Christian relic taken from Rome when the city was sacked in AD 410. According to the fifth-century historian Olympiodorus, it was taken with other sacred artefacts to the isle of Britain, as the province was considered relatively safe from the full-scale barbarian invasions threatening the rest of the Western Empire.

- If the Marian Chalice and the other relics were brought to Britain as Olympiodorus states, then their most likely destination would have been the city of Viroconium, at that time the most important Roman city in Britain. The archaeological evidence shows that the city had been rebuilt around AD 400 while other cities were being abandoned. Two centuries later, when Viroconium itself was finally sacked, its ruler Cynddylan ordered the hiding of what may have been the same relics.

- The Marian Chalice could well have sparked a legend which later inspired the medieval Grail romances. It is certainly the nearest historical equivalent to the Holy Grail yet discovered, and there is a strong possibility that it was once housed in the city of Viroconium from around AD 410 to 658. The Marian Chalice may therefore have been in Viroconium at the same time that the city served as the capital for Owain Ddantgwyn, the historical Arthur.

Chapter VII

The Emperor King

One theme that the early Grail romances all have in common is their portrayal of a Grail family: only the Fisher King (or Rich Fisher) and his line can be the Grail's guardians. This, we are told, is the family of Perceval. So what exactly is King Arthur's role? Why was he so intrinsically linked with the Grail? The answer may be found in the *Didcot Perceval*, which describes Arthur as being the head of Christ's Church. According to the story, the Round Table represented the table of the Last Supper and, like Joseph of Arimathea before him, Arthur was to sit in the place of Jesus as rightful head of the Church. As the same story says that Jesus appointed Joseph as Grail guardian, it seems to imply that Arthur is also cast in this role.

There appears to be some confusion here, for in the *Didcot Perceval* Bron is the Grail guardian. Perceval is Bron's successor and it is he who must eventually protect the Grail. The same paradoxical theme occurs in other medieval Grail romances. In *Perlesvaus* and the Vulgate *Lancelot* Arthur is as much the rightful Grail guardian as Bron or Perceval. In the Vulgate version, for instance, he is given a Grail – the book written by Christ himself. As the same romance has previously described Joseph of Arimathea as being given the cup of the Last Supper by Jesus to ordain him as head of the Church, Arthur is clearly being appointed as Joseph's successor. Not only is he given a Grail; more significantly he is being taught the inner mysteries of the Church.

But how can these romances cast Arthur in the role of Grail guardian, when Perceval and his family have the same honour? The answer to this riddle may be that the romances were derived from two separate traditions. One that the Perceval family were the Grail guardians, and the other that it was the family of Arthur. This might explain why different romances used different names for the guardian, the Rich Fisher and the

Fisher King. Perhaps Perceval and Arthur had originally been portrayed as living in different eras of history, one succeeding the other many years later. Ultimately, they were confused as having lived at the same time. The evidence for this we shall examine later. For the time being, however, we must concentrate on Arthur's role.

How might King Arthur's portrayal as Grail guardian relate to the events surrounding the life of the historical Arthur? The Marian Chalice appears to have been the historical Holy Grail, probably kept at Viroconium from 410 to 658. Arthur seemingly ruled from Viroconium from around 488, so the chalice may have been under his protection. But why do the romances also portray him as head of the Church? The answer may lie with the fact that he is also described as an emperor, for instance by the *Didcot Perceval* (see p. 35). By the late fifth century Britain was the only part of the empire free from barbarian invasion. During the historical Arthur's time, around the 480s, it appears to have been the last surviving outpost of the former Western Empire. Arthur, therefore, may well have been considered the true Roman emperor, just as the romance asserts. The *Didcot Perceval* is certainly correct in that two earlier British leaders had become Roman emperors: the British imperial governors Magnus Maximus and Constantine III who had both seized the imperial throne, in 383 and 407 respectively.

If the historical Arthur was considered to be emperor at the close of the fifth century, then there is a strong possibility that the Britons would have perceived him as head of the Church. As we have seen, even as late as the fifth century the Pope was not universally believed to be its head. When the Church was officially recognised by the Emperor Constantine the Great in the early fourth century, the emperor himself became its head. At the First General Council of the Church, held in Nicaea in Turkey in AD 325, Constantine threatened to exile any bishop who refused to agree to the newly formed Church constitution. Many Christians did not accept Constantine's self-imposed authority and were branded heretics. One by one, however, the dissenting factions either dissolved or converted to Constantine's Roman Catholicism. Successive emperors remained head of the Catholic Church, although after their failure to halt the barbarian invasions from the early fifth century, the Church hierarchy began looking to the Bishop of Rome – the Pope – as their true leader. By the final collapse of the empire in the 470s, opinion was still divided, but soon, with no more emperors, the Pope assumed absolute authority. In free Britain, however, the Church probably continued to regard the emperor as its official figurehead. We have already seen how the British Church was in severe conflict with the Roman Church in the late 420s, when Germanus was sent to re-Catholicise the country.

To discover if Arthur really was appointed emperor in Britain, we must examine the period immediately preceding him. Although anarchy threatened the island after the legions left in AD 410, in many parts of Britain, particularly the west, a Roman way of life continued until the late fifth century. Indeed, as late as 470 a British contingent fought alongside the last true Roman emperor, Romulus Augustulus, when he tried to recapture Gaul. After the failure of this campaign in 476, Romulus was defeated by the German warlord Odovacer and Rome fell. With the collapse of the empire, Britain was the last stronghold of Roman civilisation in the West.

Gildas explains that the British leader in the 470s was a Roman commander named Ambrosius Aurelianus, and it seems to have been around 488 that Arthur succeeded him as the leader of the Britons, taking up the fight against the invading Anglo-Saxons. We might, therefore, learn something of Arthur's role by knowing more about Ambrosius. He does not seem to have been simply another chieftain, but an important Roman officer.

Gildas tells us that Ambrosius' parents 'wore purple', the imperial colour. This means that they were members of the imperial royal family. Perhaps his father was the emperor himself. Might Ambrosius have been the son of Romulus Augustulus, having fled to Britain after the collapse of Rome? Records of the final days of imperial Rome are sketchy, so it is quite possible that a son of Romulus went unrecorded. However, the situation is more confusing, for there were many people claiming to be the true imperial family. In the last century of the Roman Empire, would-be emperors were constantly usurping one another with alarming regularity. Indeed, at one point no fewer than six separate individuals all claimed to be the emperor at the same time.

A clue to which emperor Ambrosius might have been related to can be found in a legend recorded by Nennius. According to the account, the British warlord Vortigern attempted to construct a fortress in the Snowdonia mountains in north Wales, but the work was constantly disrupted by a strange series of disasters. Ambrosius then appeared before Vortigern, telling him that the problems were caused by two serpents that dwelt beneath the fort's foundations. When the serpents were found, Vortigern accepted Ambrosius as his equal, offering to share his throne. Although clearly legend, it provides important clues as to Ambrosius' background. On seeing the two serpents Vortigern is moved to pay tribute to Ambrosius. The serpents must therefore be an allegorical reference concerning Ambrosius' lineage and right to rule.

The dual serpent motif is recorded in the *Notitia Dignitatum* (*circa* 420) – which contains a list of the insignia of late Roman legions and important army officers – as the personal emblem of the Roman emperor Magnus Maximus. It may therefore be to Maximus' family that the Nennius legend is linking Ambrosius.

Maximus was a British-based general who seized the imperial throne in the closing years of the fourth century. In 376 the Roman emperor Gratianus executed his main rival Theodosius on the charge of high treason. Gratianus was considered by many high-ranking soldiers to be incompetent, and Theodosius had been seen as a possible replacement. The only other threat to Gratianus came from his general Magnus Maximus, but not daring to risk another execution the emperor played safe. He ensured that Maximus remained in command of the imperial forces on the far-off island of Britain, posting him to the Segontium garrison at Caernarvon in north Wales.

It was only a few years before Gratianus made one mistake too many, and the army came close to revolt. In 383 Maximus was proclaimed emperor by the legions under his command. Taking his troops, he left Britain and sailed for the Continent. He won the support of the legions in Gaul, conquered Italy and marched on Rome. Gratianus was soon assassinated and Maximus took his place. The Eastern Empire, however, refused to recognise Maximus, instead proclaiming emperor the son of Theodosius, also named Theodosius. In the ensuing civil war Maximus was defeated and killed.

After the war the Western Empire was in tatters and Theodosius continued to rule from Constantinople. But there were many in Britain who still regarded the family of Maximus as the rightful heirs to the imperial throne. Theodosius, on the other hand, did not see them as a threat, and not wishing to risk another campaign took no action.

As Maximus' family continued to live in north Wales, Ambrosius may well have been his descendant – according to Nennius, Ambrosius came from that very area. Descent from Maximus was certainly considered important in the post-Roman era. From a ninth-century inscription on the Pillar of Eliseg, the remains of a stone cross near Llangollen in central Wales, we learn that Vortigern had married

Maximus' daughter Severa, in an attempt to legitimise his own leadership.

The Nennius story may have been an allegory regarding Ambrosius' claim to a more direct line of descent than Vortigern, who was related to the imperial family by marriage alone. It is possible that Ambrosius was descended from another of Maximus' daughters. Indeed, Gildas' description of his 'parents', rather than just his 'father', was the usual way of implying matrilineal descent in early Christian times.

According to Nennius, Vortigern was ultimately forced to abdicate and Ambrosius became the sole British leader. Sometime around 488, Arthur then succeeded Ambrosius. Was he also a member of the Maximus family? If Arthur was Owain Ddantgwyn, as our research suggests, then he was not the son of Ambrosius. The *Welsh Annals* name him as the son of a Gwynedd warlord named Enniaun Girt. It is, however, possible that, like Vortigern before him, Owain married into the Maximus dynasty. Indeed, the originator of the Arthurian romances, Geoffrey of Monmouth, says that Arthur married a Roman princess.

In 1135 Geoffrey claimed to have discovered information about Arthur's life from 'an ancient book in the old British language', and wrote that Arthur's queen had been the daughter of a Roman emperor. Geoffrey calls her Ganhumara, from which the later romances derived the more lyrical-sounding name Guinevere. Interestingly, only a few miles from Owain Ddantgwyn's capital Viroconium survives a Guinevere legend telling how after Arthur's death the queen retired to a priory close to what had been Camelot. In the most famous Arthurian romance, Thomas Malory's *Le Morte d'Arthur* (*circa* 1470), Guinevere retires to a secluded priory after Arthur's death. According to a sixteenth-century rendition of Malory's tale, it is White Ladies Prior, twelve miles to the east of Viroconium. Although the present ruins date from the Middle Ages, there may have been a prior on the site during the historical Arthurian period, as ecclesiastical buildings were often constructed on older sanctified sites.

As both Vortigern and Ambrosius seem to have married into the Maximus family, it is possible that Arthur did too. Indeed, there is historical evidence to suggest just this. As Ambrosius' successor, Arthur also appears to have employed the Maximus dual serpent as his standard. Not only has late-fifth-century royal Powysian jewellery bearing the device of two serpents been found in Shropshire but the same insignia is said to have been on Arthur's sword. *The Dream of Rhonabwy* (in *The*

Red Book of Hergest), a twelfth-century Welsh work believed to be based on an earlier Dark Age war poem, contains the oldest known description of Arthur's sword, recording it as bearing 'a design of two serpents on its golden hilt'. If the historical Arthur's sword really did bear such a device, then it may have been a symbol of imperial authority.

Arthur may have inherited this sword from his predecessors. From Roman writers we learn that leadership disputes between rival British warriors were often resolved in single combat, the victor drawing a 'sword of office' from a stone altar – a practice that may have given rise to the Arthurian sword and stone legend. The importance accredited to Excalibur in the later legends may have arisen because the sword was originally a symbol of Roman imperial authority – the sword of Maximus, the inheritance of the true emperor. Remarkably, when co-author Martin Keatman and I created a replica of such a sword, it helped to provide confirmatory evidence to link the historical Arthur with the Maximus family.

In legend, Excalibur was a huge broadsword which bestowed kingship upon the rightful heir to the British throne. But what of the historical Arthur's sword? With the help of a leading authority on post-Roman military history, Dan Shadrake of the Dark Age battle re-enactment society Britannia, we reconstructed a fifth-century sword bearing a Powysian dual serpent design.

Archaeology has demonstrated that swords of the fifth century were not the huge, heavy broadswords erroneously associated with Excalibur, but the Roman *spatha*, of slimmer design with a stunted cross guard. This double-bladed Roman cavalry sword had an overall length of about sixty centimetres, including the hilt of about fifteen centimetres. Examples include two *spathas* found at Newstead on Hadrian's Wall (now in the Museum of Antiquities, Edinburgh), and a restored *spatha* in the Rijksmuseum in Nijmegen, Holland.

A ceremonial sword blade made for a high-ranking officer would have been of highly polished iron, inlaid with the kingdom's ornamental scrolling. The sword possessed by the historical Arthur – Owain Ddantgwyn – may therefore have been etched with the Powysian scrolling, known from a fifth-century inscribed stone in the British Museum. (Each kingdom had its own unique scrolling, just as Scottish clans have their own individual tartan.)

If Arthur came from Powys, the hilt would probably have been decorated with double serpents similar to those found on late Roman jewellery discovered in central Britain. Coming from the same time and place as the historical Arthur, this ornamentation is further evidence for the double serpents being an important royal insignia of the period. These rings, neck torcs and arm bands suggest that the hilt ornamentation would have been similar to the Maximus twin serpent design in the *Notitia Dignitatum*.

Ultimately, we approached the Queen's sword-makers, Wilkinson Sword, who agreed to reconstruct the weapon. When a photograph of the sword appeared in the *Daily Telegraph*, a reader wrote to us to reveal something that neither of us had previously known. In a late Roman document called the *Vistenium* (*circa* AD 400), now in the Turkish National Museum in Ankara, there is a drawing of a sceptre made for Magnus Maximus during his brief period as emperor. Around the shaft were entwined twin serpents, identical to those on the Excalibur replica. Consequently, if Arthur's sword really had been as the research indicated, then it was decorated with the royal insignia of Magnus Maximus. In other words, Arthur had inherited a sword of office which was a symbol of imperial succession.

The Song of Llywarch the Old not only confirms that the kings of Powys saw themselves as the true emperors in the early Dark Ages, it shows that Arthur himself was indeed thought to be one. The poem was committed to writing some time around the eighth century, but refers to events seemingly described first hand in 568. In the verse where King Cynddylan orders the relics to be hidden, he is described as 'Cynddylan, vested in purple' (see p. 57). Here he is being described as an emperor, in exactly the way that Gildas describes Ambrosius' parents. Since in the same poem Cynddylan and his family are also described as 'heirs of great Arthur', it clearly implies that Arthur himself had previously been considered an emperor.

History appears to link precisely with the medieval Grail romances: in the romances Arthur is portrayed as the head of the Church, a Roman emperor, and guardian of the Grail. The historical Arthur could well have been all three: the head of the Church in Britain, considered a Roman emperor, and the guardian of the Marian Chalice. The Grail romances refer to the Grail being in the possession of the Grail family, that of either Arthur or Perceval. If the historical Grail was the Marian Chalice, then the true Grail family in the Dark Ages were seemingly the descendants of Owain Ddantgwyn.

What became of this dynasty? Although Owain's direct lineal heir

Cynddylan died fighting the Saxons, Cynddylan's sister Heledd survived. It was her descendants who became the kings of lesser Powys, the kingdom that remained free from Saxon rule in central Wales. Was it from this royal family of Powys that the medieval romancers took their story? Had they become the Grail guardians, or at least the guardians of the Marian Chalice? To answer these questions we must now attempt to trace their successors to the time the romances were written in the late twelfth century.

Summary

• One theme that the early Grail romances all have in common is their portrayal of a Grail family: only the Fisher King (or Rich Fisher) and his line can be the Grail's guardians. Although this is said to be the family of Perceval, Arthur himself is also cast in this role. The *Didcot Perceval*, the Vulgate *Lancelot* and *Perlesvaus* all portray Arthur as a Grail guardian. The Marian Chalice seems to have been the historical Holy Grail; seemingly kept at Viroconium from around 410 to 658. If Arthur had ruled from Viroconium from around the 480s, the chalice may actually have been under his protection.

• The *Didcot Perceval* also describes Arthur as a Roman emperor. By the historical Arthur's time, around the 480s, Britain appears to have been the last surviving outpost of the Western Empire. Arthur, as the leader of the Britons, may therefore have been considered the true emperor.

• *The Dream of Rhonabwy*, a twelfth-century Welsh work believed to be based on an earlier Dark Age war poem, contains the oldest known description of Arthur's sword, recording it as bearing 'a design of two serpents on its golden hilt'. If the historical Arthur's sword really did bear such a device, then it may have been a symbol of imperial authority. The *Notitia Dignitatum* (*circa* 420) records the dual serpent motif as the personal emblem of the fourth-century Roman emperor Magnus Maximus.

• *The Song of Llywarch the Old* not only confirms that the kings of Powys saw themselves as the true emperors in the early Dark Ages, it shows that Arthur himself was thought to be one. The poem was committed to writing some time around the eighth century, but refers to events seemingly described first hand in 568. In one verse King Cynddylan is described as 'Cynddylan, vested in purple', the colour exclusively reserved for the Roman emperors. As the same poem describes Cynddylan and his family as 'heirs of great Arthur', it suggests that Arthur himself had previously been considered an emperor.

• The *Didcot Perceval* describes Arthur not only as an emperor, but as head of Christ's Church. If the historical Arthur was seen as emperor at the close of the fifth century, then there is a strong possibility that the Britons would have considered him head of the Church. In the late Roman Empire the emperor was thought by many to be head of the Catholic Church.

• In the romances Arthur is portrayed as the head of the Church, a Roman emperor, and guardian of the Grail. The historical Arthur could well have been all three: the head of the Church in Britain, considered a Roman emperor, and the guardian of the Marian Chalice. The Grail romances refer to the Grail being in the possession of the Grail family. If the historical Grail was the Marian Chalice, then the true Grail family in the Dark Ages were seemingly the descendants of Owain Ddantgwyn.

Chapter VIII

The Heirs of Arthur

When Owain Ddantgwyn died, around AD 520, civil war appears to have broken out between his rival heirs, his son Cuneglasus, and his nephew Maglocunus. As this is approximately the time that archaeology has discovered Viroconium to have been abandoned for a few decades, Cuneglasus probably left the capital for a more defensible site, perhaps the Iron Age hill fort on nearby Wrekin Hill. Within a decade or two, the Powysians reoccupied Viroconium, but, as the latest phase of excavations has revealed, the city was plundered by the Saxons in the mid seventh century. This must have been the time of Owain's great-great-grandson Cynddylan, and the events described in *The Song of Llywarch the Old*. By the seventh century Britain moved progressively into a period of recorded history. The gradual conversion of the Anglo-Saxons to Christianity led to the mass founding of monasteries, and the subsequent spread of writing skills. It is therefore far easier to examine the later Dark Ages than the historical Arthurian era.

Cynddylan was the last of Owain's direct descendants to rule in greater Powys, by which time Britain had fragmented into a number of feuding kingdoms, and the Anglo-Saxons had invaded much of the country. The kingdom of Powys, in the west Midlands and central Wales, was virtually all that remained of what had been Arthur's Britain. In order to defend his kingdom against the Northumbrian Saxons, who were attacking from the north, Cynddylan formed an alliance with Penda of Mercia (an Anglo-Saxon kingdom which covered the east Midlands), and Aethelhere of East Anglia (centred in Norfolk and Suffolk). However, after the defeat of Penda and Aethelhere in 655 Powys stood alone.

With the British of Powys in retreat, *The Song of Llywarch the Old* relates how Cynddylan is killed and his kingdom sacked. During an elegy on Cynddylan's death, the poem describes his pillaged court being seen below *Dinlle Wrecon*, probably the Wrekin which overlooked Viroconium. Now Viroconium was abandoned for the final time and the British fled west into the Shropshire marshes and central Wales.

This final defeat of Cynddylan and the sacking of Powys occurred around 658, and was probably the event referred to in the *Welsh Annals*, which record that Oswy of Northumbria plundered the kingdom. The British of Shropshire were certainly conquered by the Anglo-Saxons by 661, as the people of the Wrekin district are entered in the *Tribal Hidage*, a contemporary census of Mercian-held territories. Also, a ford over the Severn near Melverley, ten miles west of Shrewsbury, is recorded as 'Wulfhere's Ford', Wulfhere being the Anglo-Saxon ruler by 660.

Named after the Northumbrian king Oswy, who defeated the Britons in Shropshire, Oswestry hill fort, twelve miles north-west of Shrewsbury, was probably the site of Cynddylan's last stand. Unfortunately, Cynddylan's direct descendants are difficult to trace, and with his death we temporarily lose the trail of the Arthurian blood line.

Cynddylan must have been buried within a few years of his old ally Aethelhere of East Anglia, who died fighting Oswy about 655. The burial site of the East Anglian kings has been discovered at Sutton Hoo near Ipswich. Indeed, Aethelhere himself is probably the famous 'Sutton Hoo Man', whose burial mound was excavated in 1939. The Sutton Hoo dig revealed one of the richest archaeological finds in Europe: an entire Anglo-Saxon ship, along with jewellery, ornaments and other family treasures, now restored and on display at the British Museum. No British equivalent has yet been discovered. However, as Cynddylan is described in *The Song of Llywarch the Old* as being buried at the Churches of Bassa, perhaps the Berth at modern Baschurch may hold such a discovery for the future. Unfortunately, financial restraints prevent excavation there at present.

Continuing to trace the descendants of Owain Ddantgwyn, we turn to the Welsh genealogies, a series of Welsh family trees drawn up between the ninth and twelfth centuries. Some include the names of Owain Ddantgwyn and his son Cuneglasus. Owain's other sons – Meiryawn, Seiryoel and Einyawn – are named in a series of genealogies attached to the tenth-century *Welsh Annals* in the British Library. Unfortunately, other than their immediate offspring, nothing is recorded of their descendants.

Returning to Owain's eldest son Cuneglasus, we discover three separate genealogies which record the lineage of a ninth-century Welsh ruler, Hywel ap Caradoc. All three, including the earliest, in the *Welsh Annals*, give Hywel's descent from Cuneglasus' son Meic. By Hywel's time, around 830, the native Britons had been reduced to two pockets of resistance, in Wales and Cornwall. Ultimately, even Cornwall was conceded to the Anglo-Saxons, in 926, leaving only the area we now call Wales as the surviving homeland of the native Britons. The Anglo-Saxons referred to the native Britons as 'Welsh', from the Saxon word *weala* meaning foreigners, and their own territory they called England (Angle land).

Wales itself fragmented into many small kingdoms, of which Hywel ruled Rhos, on the north coast of Wales in modern Clwyd. Although he left no heir, Hywel did leave what may be another intriguing legacy of the Arthurian era. The mountain hill fort from which he ruled, on Bryn Euryn near Llandrillo, was called Dinarth – the 'Fort of the Bear'. As it appears from Gildas that Cuneglasus adopted his father's battle name, the Bear, it would seem that this same name may have continued in the family for at least three centuries.

The monk Nennius, author of the *Historia Brittonum* (the oldest surviving account of Arthur's battles), was not only a contemporary of Hywel, he also appears to have come from Bangor, only a few miles from Rhos. It may therefore have been from this direct descendant of the historical Arthur that Nennius obtained his information concerning Arthur's life.

We pick up the Arthurian trail in the Vale of Llangollen in central Wales. Here stands the Pillar of Eliseg, erected around 850 by the Powys king Cyngen. Its inscription celebrated Cyngen's line of descent from Maximus, telling how Vortigern married the emperor's daughter Severa, and through their son Britu their line ran unbroken down to Cyngen. One name on the Pillar suggests that Cynddylan's brother-in-law ruled lesser Powys after 658. From *The Song of Llywarch the Old* we learn that after her flight from the White Town, Cynddylan's sister Heledd married a prince named Concenn, a name recorded on the Pillar of Eliseg as the king of Powys around the same period. It would therefore seem that with Cynddylan's death, the rulership of Powys passed via his sister Heledd, the great-great-granddaughter of Owain Ddantgwyn, and ultimately through her to Cyngen by the mid ninth century.

The *Welsh Annals* record Cyngen's death on a visit to Rome in the mid 850s, during a rash attempt to claim the title of Holy Roman Emperor.

After the fall of the Western Empire, Rome remained the centre of Catholic Christianity, and in 800 the Frankish king Charlemagne decided to utilise its influence. The Pope crowned him as emperor, in return for accepting Catholicism as the State religion. Charlemagne's empire, which covered parts of Italy, France and Germany, became known as the Holy Roman Empire, and his successors inherited the title of Holy Roman Emperor. It seems that around 855 Cyngen travelled to Rome to dispute this claim.

He failed, and was executed by the Holy Roman Emperor, Louis II. The ninth-century Italian writer Ambrose Marca describes how Cyngen took an imperial sceptre to the Pope to prove his claim. Decorated with twin serpents, it was apparently the sceptre of Maximus described in the fifth-century *Vistenium* (see Chapter VII). What happened to the sceptre itself is a mystery but the story demonstrates once again that the family of Owain Ddantgwyn still considered themselves to be descendants of Maximus, and true Roman emperors.

As Cyngen died with no son to succeed him, the hereditary line appears to end. However, returning to 658 and Cynddylan, who also had no surviving son, we discover that the blood line continued through his cousin Cynwise, and an Anglo-Saxon dynasty. The British Library's *Cotton Vespasian* (a Saxon document compiled around 900) shows that Cynwise married Penda, Cynddylan's Mercian ally. After Penda's death in 658, their son Wulfhere formed a pact with the Northumbrian king, Oswy, and continued to rule Mercia as an Anglo-Saxon kingdom.

Wulfhere's hereditary line can be traced for 250 years, until it ends with the last Mercian king, Ethelred, in the early tenth century. Ethelred died without an heir, and so his wife Ethelfleda became queen, winning fame throughout Britain for defeating the invading Danes. In 914 Ethelfleda fortified the city of Warwick against the Danes. Although construction of the present Warwick Castle did not begin until the eleventh or twelfth century, this was the first fortified building on the site. The mound on which this earliest fort is thought to have stood is known as Ethelfleda's Mound, and lies within the grounds of the present Warwick Castle.

Ethelfleda's child from a second marriage became the Mercian leader. Subject to the Wessex king Athelstan, he and his descendants were demoted from kings of Mercia to earls of Warwick. However, although descended from Ethelfleda, the earls of Warwick were not related to Ethelred, the last of the Owain Ddantgwyn line.

Although we confront another termination in the blood line, we do find what may be a surviving legacy of the Arthurian era. The crest of the medieval earls of Warwick is a bear holding a large ragged staff. Its origins are obscure, but the bear is generally thought to have been the emblem of the Saxon kings of Mercia, of whom Ethelred was the last. As 'Bear' seems to have been Owain's battle name, and the origin of the name Arthur, the Mercian kings may have adopted this title once their dynasty merged with that of the Powysian kings.

The earliest surviving reference to the origin of the Warwick crest supports its link with the historical Arthur. According to John Rous, a fifteenth-century Warwick priest, the bear device was first adopted by Arthgallus, an ancient earl of Warwick and one of King Arthur's knights. Although clearly legend, Rous' account may contain an element of truth. In his book, the *Rous Rol* (now in the British Library), written around 1480, he explains that *arth* is Welsh for 'bear'; the reason for the crest. He fails, however, to point out that in Welsh *gallus* means 'mighty'. Inadvertently, Rous seems to have discovered that the Warwick crest originated from someone called the 'Mighty Bear', who was somehow connected with Arthur. As there is no historical record of Arthgallus, it is possible that the name originally referred to Arthur himself.

It would support the Arthur/Warwick bear theory if Rous had simply written that the crest originated with a character called Arthgallus, but his association of Arthgallus with King Arthur renders the argument all the more compelling. Moreover, Rous' source material further supports the case, for he refers to a 'Welsh chronicle from the land of Powys', the kingdom of the historical King Arthur. It would therefore seem that Rous learned of both Arthgallus' association with Warwick and the origin of the bear crest in this Welsh Powysian chronicle.

As we have seen, it seems that Owain's descendants continued to inherit the battle name the Bear. The Saxon line of the family may also have used the name, which by medieval times had become an heraldic crest. Indeed, many medieval crests originated in this way. For instance, the sixth-century Cornish warlord Constantine was known as the Lion, and by the twelfth century the dukes of Cornwall had adopted the lion as their heraldic device.

Rous also tells us that Warwick was the site of Arthur's court, implying that the castle was Camelot itself. Although Warwick could not have been the seat of the historical Arthur, it may well have been where the romances originally set the scene for Camelot. The Arthurian story we know today is chiefly the work of Sir Thomas Malory, a fifteenth-century English writer from Newbold Revel in Warwickshire. Around 1480 Malory collected together scores of medieval tales concerning the legendary King Arthur, and compiled one epic tale of his life, *Le Morte d'Arthur*. Although the early medieval writers seem uncertain where Camelot is situated, Malory associates it with the Hampshire city of Winchester. Significantly, Rous' work, placing Camelot at Warwick, was written around 1480 – the same year as Malory placed it at Winchester. Could Warwick Castle therefore have been the traditional site of Camelot before it was accepted as Winchester?

Malory's publisher William Caxton, in his preface to *Le Morte d'Arthur*, actually writes that in his opinion Winchester was not the site of Camelot. Had Malory initially based his Camelot on Warwick Castle, subsequently changing it to Winchester? As Malory knew Rous (he mentions him in his writings), and lived just a few miles from Warwick Castle, it is almost certain that he would have known of Warwick's Camelot claim. So why did Malory fail to include Warwick Castle in his work?

Sir Thomas Malory had fought in the Wars of the Roses, serving as a knight in the Earl of Warwick's army. Warwick's influence on the Yorkist side, in support of Edward IV, earned him the nickname 'the King Maker'. However, in 1470 he changed sides, exiled Edward, and placed the Lancastrian Henry VI on the throne. Along with others who continued to support Edward, Malory was arrested and incarcerated in Newgate Prison, where he was to write *Le Morte d'Arthur*. Here may lie the answer to Malory's Camelot's setting. As the Earl of Warwick had betrayed King Edward, it is possible that as Edward's supporter Malory would have relocated Camelot, replacing Warwick's seat with Edward's own castle at Winchester.

Another line of Owain Ddantgwyn descendants leads us to one of the greatest mysteries in Welsh history – the enigma of Owain Glendower.

According to a medieval Powys genealogy (discovered in St Asaph Abbey by the Welsh antiquarian Edward Lhwyd in 1696), when Cyngen of Powys died without issue about 855, his sister Nest's son Rhodri Mawr became king of Powys. His descendants were therefore of the Owain Ddantgwyn blood line. In 1400 Rhodri's direct descendant Owain Glendower was ruling in what was left of Powys. By the fourteenth century, however, the Normans had succeeded where the

Saxons had failed: they had conquered Wales, leaving Owain Glendower merely a lord in the Norman province of Powys. Subjected to the authority of the English king Henry IV, it was not long before Owain Glendower rebelled, and was proclaimed King of Wales by his followers.

By 1405 he had raised an army from every part of the country, making his headquarters at Harlech Castle. However, the following year Henry IV retook Harlech, and Owain Glendower retreated into the mountains. By 1413 the last of the rebels had surrendered, but what became of Owain Glendower himself has remained a mystery. His followers never betrayed him, he was never captured, and his death was never recorded.

During the uprising, Owain Glendower claimed descent from King Arthur, and led his troops beneath a banner bearing a golden dragon. Although his claim was never taken seriously by the English, Glendower seems to have been justified in this assertion. If Owain Ddantgwyn was the historical Arthur, then Owain Glendower was Arthur's direct descendant. Moreover, he employed an emblem reminiscent of the Arthurian era, nine centuries earlier. But Glendower shares more in common with the historical Arthur than simply his banner and name. According to the sixteenth-century Welsh poet Gruffudd Hiraethog, Glendower still sleeps, awaiting the day that he will return to free Wales from English rule – a similar legend to that which surrounded the mystery of Arthur's death.

What really happened to Owain Glendower will probably never be known, although we can make an informed guess. In 1414, while he was in hiding, his surviving heir, his daughter Alice, married Sir John Scudamore of Kentchurch Court in Herefordshire. A legend survives telling how Glendower died in a secret room at his daughter's home. It may well be based on truth: a few years ago workmen renovating Kentchurch Court discovered a secret chamber, bricked up centuries ago behind wooden panelling.

The Owain Ddantgwyn blood line did not die with Owain Glendower: his daughter Alice had a son, whose present-day descendant, John Scudamore, is the current owner of Kentchurch Court.

There is one last line of descent which returns us directly to the Grail romances. According to the Lhwyd genealogy mentioned above, in 855, when King Cyngen of Powys died without issue, his second sister Cynddia married Ynyr, a prince of Gwent. The same genealogy traces the line directly to a Welsh baron, Cadfarch, whose daughter married the

Norman baron Trevor, the Earl of Hereford, in the late eleventh century. Their sole heir, their daughter Lynette, then married another Norman baron, Payne Peveril, who had fought alongside William the Conqueror at the battle of Hastings in 1966. So who was the head of the Peveril family around the year 1200 when the romances were written?

Payne Peveril's granddaughter and sole heir, Mellet, married a certain Fulk Fitz Warine; their son, also called Fulk, was baron of Whittington Castle in Shropshire at the close of the twelfth century. It is with Fulk Fitz Warine that we return to the Grail story. A prose romance, anonymously written around 1260, included the discovery of the Grail by the man who it claimed was the true heir of King Arthur. In this story, *Fulke le Fitz Waryn*, it is not Perceval, Gawain, or any of the other familiar Knights of the Round Table who discovers the Grail, but Fulk Fitz Warine, whom the story portrays as Arthur's living heir.

Fulk Fitz Warine was the direct descendant of Owain Ddantgwyn. Owain Ddantgwyn seems to have been the historical Arthur, and his family seem to have been the guardians of the historical Grail, the Marian Chalice. Remarkably, here was a Grail romance written within a few years of the originals, claiming not only that Fulk Fitz Warine was a direct descendant of Arthur, but that he was the true guardian of the Holy Grail.

Summary

- In the mid seventh century Cynddylan was the last of Owain Ddantgwyn's direct descendants to rule in Shropshire, by which time Britain had fragmented into a number of feuding kingdoms, and the Anglo-Saxons had invaded much of the country. It would seem that on Cynddylan's death the rulership of Powys passed via his sister Heledd, the great-great-granddaughter of Owain Ddantgwyn. From *The Song of Llywarch the Old*, we learn that after the Britons' flight from Shropshire into mid Wales, Heledd married a Welsh prince named Concenn.

- The ninth-century Pillar of Eliseg, in the Vale of Llangollen in central Wales, records Concenn's descendants down to a King Cyngen in the mid ninth century. The *Welsh Annals* record Cyngen's death on a visit to Rome in the 850s, during a rash attempt to claim the title of Holy Roman Emperor.

- According to a medieval Powys genealogy (discovered in St Asaph Abbey by the Welsh antiquarian Edward Llwyd in 1696), when Cyngen of Powys died without issue around 855, his sister Cynddia married Ynyr, a prince of Gwent. The same genealogy traces the line directly to a Welsh baron, Cadfarch, whose daughter married the Norman baron Trevor, the Earl of Hereford, in the late eleventh century. Their sole heir, their daughter Lynette, then married another Norman baron, Payne Peveril, who had fought alongside William the Conqueror at the battle of Hastings in 1066.

- Payne Peveril's granddaughter and sole heir, Mellet, married a Fulk Fitz Warine, and their son, also called Fulk, was baron of Whittington Castle in Shropshire at the close of the twelfth century. It is with Fulk Fitz Warine that we return to the Grail story. A prose romance, anonymously written around 1260, included the discovery of the Grail by the man who it claimed was the true heir of King Arthur. In this story, *Fulke le Fitz Waryn*, it is not Perceval, Gawain, or any of the other familiar Knights of the Round Table who discovers the Grail, but Fulk Fitz Warine, whom the story portrays as Arthur's living heir.

Chapter IX

Fulk Fitz Warine

Fulk Fitz Warine was a rebel baron during the reign of King John. Born in the 1170s, he became lord of Whittington in Shropshire on the death of his father in 1197. However, in 1200 a rival lord successfully claimed Whittington Castle and Fulk was outlawed on a trumped-up charge of treason. For the next three years he fought against King John in the Shropshire Marches and north-central Wales. Pardoned in 1203, he re-inherited Whittington Castle, although in 1215 he again rebelled in support of the baronial revolt which led to the signing of the Magna Carta. He ultimately made peace with John's successor Henry III in 1217 and eventually died somewhere around the year 1256. (The life of Fulk Fitz Warine was outlined by the antiquarian R. W. Eyton in his *Antiquities of Shropshire* in 1860.)

After his death, Fulk became the focus of many legends and folk tales, and by the mid 1200s a romance of his life had been composed by an anonymous author. John Leland references the romance in his *Collectanea*, during the reign of Henry VIII, referring to it as 'an old French history in rhyme of the acts of the Warines'. This seems to have been the romance *Fulke le Fitz Waryn*, which still survives in the British Library in a manuscript known as the *Historia Rerum Anglicarum*. From the Anglo-Norman style of its French, it appears to have been composed in the mid thirteenth century, probably before the death of Fulk's son at the Battle of Lewes in 1265, as he is said in the author's preface to still be alive.

Fulke le Fitz Waryn focuses mainly on Fulk's life in the three years between 1200 and 1203, when he was engaged in a guerrilla campaign against King John. The story opens with Fulk being portrayed as a descendant and rightful heir of King Arthur:

He shall have such great force and virtue.
But we know that Merlin
Said it for Fulk Fitz Warine;
For each of you may be sure
That in the time of King Arthur,
That was called White Land.

We are told that Fulk must repossess the White Land of the Welsh Borders which was once the land of Arthur, but that to accomplish this he must first recover the Grail. Fulk eventually discovers the Grail in a chapel adjoining his castle at Whittington, and on his deathbed asks for it to be placed in a priory he founded in nearby Alberbury.

We have seen how the Grail romances describe the Grail kingdom as the White Land, and how the kingdom of Powys was called the White Land in Dark Age Welsh poetry. It is therefore not surprising to discover that Fulk's castle at Whittington stands in what was once the heart of Dark Age Powys, about twenty miles to the north-west of Shrewsbury. This reference to the White Land suggests that the author of *Fulke le Fitz Waryn* must either have been familiar with the Grail romances, written just a few years before, or have had access to some separate, earlier material. Moreover, we are told the name of Arthur's capital:

It was the White Town
Which is now called Whittington

We have seen how in *The Song of Llywarch the Old* Viroconium is the White Town. However, the author of *Fulke le Fitz Waryn* is telling us that Whittington, where Fulk's castle stands, is the White Town. Whittington is now in Shropshire, and until the seventh century the whole of Shropshire formed part of the British kingdom of Powys. Although the Roman city of Viroconium was the original White Town, it seems that the same name was applied to the new Powys capital once Viroconium was abandoned in 658. From the *Tribal Hidage*, the Saxon taxation document compiled in the 660s, we find reference to the new capital of the reduced kingdom of Powys. It is described as being near Oswestry, at the head of the Great March. This is precisely the location of Whittington, in the Welsh border marshes, about three miles east of Oswestry. We know from the Domesday Book, compiled for William the Conqueror in the late eleventh century, that Whittington had been the name the Saxons had used for the town. Indeed, Whittington is derived directly from the English words 'White Town'.

The *Anglo-Saxon Chronicle* records that Whittington was taken from the Britons when the Mercian king Offa advanced westwards in the late eighth century. After capturing the town Offa built a huge earthwork, now known as Offa's Dyke, to keep the Britons inside Wales. Thereafter, the kings of Powys made their new capital at Dinas Bran, a hilltop fort near Llangollen, a few miles to the west of Whittington. Whittington was thus the last Powys capital on what became English soil. It seems therefore that as lord of Whittington, Fulk was envisaged as a king of ancient Powys. Indeed, as we have seen, he did descend directly from its Dark Age rulers, although by his time the descendants of Rhodri Mawr were ruling in Welsh Powys (see Chapter VIII).

Fulke le Fitz Waryn does not portray Fulk merely as the heir of any Powysian king, however, but of King Arthur himself. Just like Arthur, the coming of Fulk has been prophesied by Merlin:

> From that country the wolf issued,
> As the wise Merlin says,
> And the twelve sharp teeth
> We have recognised by his shield.
> He carried a shield indented,
> As the sayers have devised;
> In the shield are twelve teeth
> Of gules [gold] and of argent [silver].

Fulk's shield bears a design of twelve teeth, six above, six below, resembling the open mouth of an angry wolf. This, says Merlin, is the hero's mark:

> A wolf will come from the White Land;
> Twelve teeth he shall have sharp,
> Six beneath and six above.

Fulke le Fitz Waryn is a combination of historical events surrounding the life of the hero, merged with romantic fiction. In the fabulous sections of the story Fulk goes in search of the Grail, where he becomes an Arthurian-style knight, fighting dragons, rescuing damsels and outwitting witches. On a mysterious island he meets a shepherd, the porter to a magic castle cut into the mountain rocks. In order to enter the castle, Fulk is made to prove his worth by playing a bizarre game of chess with gold and silver pieces. Each time he is about to win the game, the shepherd's seven brothers, dressed as jesters, successfully distract him. Fulk finally loses his patience and runs them through with his sword.

With the jesters dead, Fulk enters the castle to discover an old woman and seven maidens, guardians of a magical horn which has the power to summon help in times of danger. Taking the horn Fulk leaves the island, travels to a land in the frozen north, defeats two serpents, rescues a damsel in distress, and finally returns home.

The story is not just similar to an Arthurian tale; Fulk's quest is almost identical to the Arthurian tales of early Welsh literature. The early Welsh stories *The Dialogue of Arthur*, *The Dream of Rhonabwy*, *Culhwch and Olwen* and *The Spoils of Annwn* all contain direct comparisons with episodes from *Fulke le Fitz Waryn*. Fulk's castle is on the Welsh/Shropshire border, from where 'he will drive away the boar'. *The Dream of Rhonabwy* sites Arthur's court precisely on the Welsh/Shropshire border, and *Culhwch and Olwen* tells of Arthur hunting down a boar. Fulk's final 'stronghold' is 'in the water', as is Arthur's on the isle of Avalon. To succeed Fulk must better an opponent in a bizarre game of chess, as must Arthur in *The Dream of Rhonabwy*. To gain entrance to the enchanted castle Fulk must outwit the shepherd guardian before being allowed inside, the same task set for Arthur in *The Dialogue of Arthur*.

Fulk's voyage across the western sea to the mysterious island where he discovers the magic horn is very similar to *The Spoils of Annwn*. The theme of this tale is a raid by Arthur and his men into the magical land of Annwn to steal a magical cauldron. In *Fulke le Fitz Waryn* the horn has replaced the cauldron, but just like the cauldron, it is guarded by a wise woman and a community of maidens.

Fulk's final adventure before he makes his peace with the king is to decapitate a giant in Ireland, returning with his head to Whittington Castle. Again this appears to be alluding to the Arthurian legend as it appears in a cycle of Welsh poems called the Triads. Taking their name from their groupings of themes or characters into threes, the Triads served as a mnemonic device summarising Welsh folklore. They were anonymously committed to writing during the Middle Ages by a group of Welsh writers, probably in the hope of preserving some of the Welsh oral tradition that was rapidly being lost. Not really poems in the true sense, they are essentially outlines of what were obviously more detailed sagas. King Arthur is referenced in a series called *The Triads of Britain*, which also include a number of known historical characters from the Dark Ages. (Although dispersed through many Welsh manuscripts, *The Triads of Britain* were not brought together in one printed text until 1567. The surviving copy, *Y Diarebion Camberac*, is now in the British Library.)

The Triads are intriguing in that Arthur is not always depicted as the epitome of majestic virtue – in fact, far from it. In *The Three Wicked Uncoverings* he is blamed for the ultimate defeat of the Britons, being guilty of removing the head of the god Bran that had been buried on London's Tower Hill as a talisman against foreign invasion.

The Norman keep of the Tower of London was (and still is) called the White Tower. Consequently, the original story may have referred to the White Tower in the White Town, as Fulk's castle is called in *Fulke le Fitz Waryn*. Moreover, Fulk's castle is even called the Castle of Bran in the opening verses of *Fulke le Fitz Waryn*. By returning the head of the giant, presumably Bran, it appears that Fulk is being portrayed as setting right Arthur's mistake.

Even the story of Fulk overcoming the two serpents is reminiscent of Ambrosius' task in Nennius' account. It may be alluding to Fulk's right to inherit the insignia of the Arthurian royal family, the dual serpents. In conclusion, the author of *Fulke le Fitz Waryn* clearly had access to earlier Arthurian material. Moreover, in the romance we discover what may well be verses from a lost Arthurian poem.

The author continually quotes verses from a poem in order to prove that they foretell the coming of Fulk Fitz Warine. The main text of *Fulke le Fitz Waryn* is written in Anglo-Norman French prose, but these poetic verses are in medieval Welsh. Linguistic analysis indicates that the Welsh sections date from the early twelfth century and seem, therefore, to be from an early romance which the author of *Fulke le Fitz Waryn* chose to include in its original language. Evidently, the author was portraying Fulk as an Arthurian successor in order to appeal to the Welsh, themselves in rebellion against the English king at the time the story was composed (*circa* 1260). As Fulk had successfully fought alongside Welsh barons in the early thirteenth century, the author apparently intended to influence the Midland barons and the Welsh princes to again join forces to defeat King Henry III.

The Welsh poem in *Fulke le Fitz Waryn* is now believed to be part of a lost medieval Welsh romance called the *Peveril*, named after its hero Payne Peveril, Fulk's great-grandfather. It is with the *Peveril* sections of *Fulke le Fitz Waryn* that the mystery of the Grail romances may be solved. It could be all that remains of the oldest Grail romance of all – the story upon which all the rest were based. Incredibly, the *Peveril* may reveal an historical Perceval and an historical Grail castle.

Summary

- Fulk Fitz Warine was an historical figure who became lord of Whittington in Shropshire in 1197. However, a rival lord claimed the estate and had Fulk outlawed on a trumped-up charge of treason. For three years Fulk fought against King John in the Shropshire Marches and north-central Wales, until he was eventually pardoned and reinstated at Whittington Castle.

- Shortly after his death, in the mid-1200s, a romance of his life was composed by an anonymous author. Known as *Fulke le Fitz Waryn*, it portrays Fulk as the descendant and rightful heir of King Arthur. In the romance we are told that Fulk must repossess the White Land, but to accomplish this he must first recover the Grail. He eventually discovers the Grail in a chapel adjoining Whittington Castle, and on his deathbed asks for it to be placed in a priory he founded in nearby Alberbury.

- Like the Grail romances, *Fulke le Fitz Waryn* names Arthur's capital as 'the White Town', which the author tells us is Whittington. Although the Roman city of Viroconium was the original White Town, it seems that the same name was applied to Whittington, the new Powys capital after Viroconium was abandoned when the Britons retreated west in 658. The name Whittington is derived directly from the English words 'White Town'.

- In *Fulke le Fitz Waryn* we discover what may well be verses from a lost Arthurian poem. The author continually quotes verses from this poem in order to prove that they foretell the coming of Fulk Fitz Warine. The main text of the romance is written in Anglo-Norman French prose, but these poetic verses are in medieval Welsh. Linguistic analysis indicates that the Welsh sections date from the early twelfth century and seem, therefore, to be from an early Arthurian romance.

- The Welsh poem in *Fulke le Fitz Waryn* is now believed to be part of a lost medieval Welsh romance called the *Peveril*, named after its hero Payne Peveril, Fulk's great-grandfather. It is with the *Peveril* sections of *Fulke le Fitz Waryn* that the mystery of the Grail romances may be solved. It could be all that remains of the oldest Grail romance of all – the story upon which all the rest were based.

Chapter X

The Historical Perceval

Although much within the Grail romances is clearly fictitious – or at least allegorical – like Arthur, there may have been an historical character upon whom the legendary Perceval was based. A passage in the *Didcot Perceval* contains a vital clue that ultimately leads us to just such a figure. According to its anonymous author, the original Grail story had been taken from 'a book in the British language, which was dictated to Brother Blayse'. Who was this mysterious Brother Blayse?

A number of modern literary scholars have proposed that the author may have been a monk with the same name, recorded at the abbey of St Asaph in north Wales in the late eleventh century. Indeed, St Asaph is the very see to which Geoffrey of Monmouth was appointed bishop shortly after completing his *History of the Kings of Britain* around 1135. Some historians have gone so far as to suggest that the book from which Geoffrey claims to have taken his own work – 'a book in the ancient British Language' – was written, or at least translated, by Blayse himself.

If the Blayse named in the *Didcot Perceval* is the eleventh-century Welsh monk, however, then the author of the romance had placed him out of time. According to him, Blayse was a contemporary of both Merlin and Perceval. But, if this Blayse was the St Asaph monk of the late eleventh century, he lived some six centuries after the historical Arthurian period.

As discussed, it is possible that the medieval Grail story originated with two separate traditions, one holding that Perceval's family were the true Grail guardians, the other that this honour belonged to the family of Arthur. If there was an historical Perceval, perhaps he and Arthur lived during different eras, later being confused as living at the same time. If Blayse, the St Asaph monk, really was the author of the original Grail romance, then perhaps the historical Perceval was his contemporary. There has certainly been no historical evidence that anyone fitting Perceval's profile ever lived during the late fifth century.

Was there an historical figure, contemporary with the St Asaph Blayse, upon whom the story of Perceval was based? In the *Didcot Perceval*, it may be recalled, we learn the following about the Grail family:

> So know that the Grail was given into the hands of Joseph, and upon his death he left it to his brother-in-law who had the name of Bron. And this Bron had twelve sons, one of whom was named Alain li Gros. And the Fisher King commanded him to be the guardian of his brothers. This Alain has come to this land from Judea, just as Our Lord has commanded him . . . And well you may know that Alain li Gros was the father of Perceval, and for the merit of Bron his grandfather who is called the Fisher King.

The author is certainly confusing two different eras here. Joseph of Arimathea had lived in the first century, and the Arthurian period during which Perceval is said to live was over four hundred years later. The author seemd to have conflated time for the purpose of his story. The situation is further confused in that neither Arthur nor Joseph was a contemporary of Blayse, the St Asaph monk. So were Bron, Alain and Perceval based on historical figures contemporary with Blayse in the late eleventh century?

In *Fulke le Fitz Waryn* there is compelling evidence that the legend of Perceval orginated with an historical figure who was Blayse's contemporary in the late eleventh century. The romance begins the story a hundred years before Fulk's time, concentrating on Fulk's great-grandfather Payne Peveril. William the Conqueror, having recently been crowned king of England, is travelling the country:

> The king apparelled himself very richly, and came with a great host into the county of Shrewsbury . . . When King William approached the hills and valleys of Wales, he saw a town, formally enclosed with high walls, which was all burnt and ruined . . . Then the king inquired of a Briton what was the name of the town and how it came to be so named. 'Sire,' said the Briton, 'I will tell you. The castle was formally called Castle Bran, but now it is called the Old

March . . . King Bran, the son of Donwal, caused the city to be rebuilt . . . and the town which is about it is still called White Town, in English Whittington.'

Fulke le Fitz Waryn continues with William rewarding Payne Peveril for his past services by making him lord of Whittington. Payne Peveril, who we are told is the son of an Alan le Crux, then builds 'the White Castle' at the centre of the town.

In the story Payne Peveril bears remarkable similarities to Perceval in the Grail romances. Not only is his name – Peveril – similiar to Perceval, but he was the son of an Alan le Crux. In the *Didcot Perceval* Perceval's father is called Alain li Gros. (*Crux* is Latin for cross, and *groes* is Welsh for cross.) Payne Peveril's castle is called 'the White Castle', the name applied to Perceval's Grail castle in *Perlesvaus*. According to the *Fulke* romance Payne Peveril's castle had once belonged to someone named Bran, and nearly all the Grail romances give the Fisher King a very similar name – Bron. Also, we are told that Bran's castle was called the 'Old March', exactly the name used for the Fisher King's castle in the Vulgate *Lancelot*. Finally, three of the romances place the Grail castle in or near 'the White Town', and Payne Peveril's castle was in the White Town of Whittington.

Was Payne Peveril the historical Perceval? His life certainly pre-dates Perceval's first appearance in the Arthurian romances. Perhaps these startling similarities were merely due to the author of *Fulke le Fitz Waryn*, written around 1260, having lifted his character from the *Didcot Perceval*, composed about sixty years earlier. However, this seems highly unlikely: Payne Peveril and his father were not fictional characters, they were real historical figures. Both their names and Payne Peveril's lordship of Whittington are recorded in the Domesday Book and in the twelfth-century *Feet of Fines*. Equally, not only was Peveril a contemporary of the St Asaph Blayse, but the records of St Asaph Abbey show that Blayse actually became the priest of Whittington in 1090. It is surely beyond coincidence that the most likely author of the original Grail story, adapted by the author of the *Didcot Perceval*, was Payne Peveril's personal chaplain.

The reference to Payne Peveril in *Fulke le Fitz Waryn* seem to have been taken from the Welsh *Peveril* poem composed around 1100 – a poem that was probably written by Blayse himself. It was even in his native, contemporary tongue. The *Peveril* was written in early-twelfth-

ABOVE. The ruins of Viroconium – the historical Camelot.

BELOW. Travail's Acre – the burial site of the historical Arthur.

ABOVE. Whittington Castle – the Grail castle in the earliest Grail romance.

BELOW. The site of the Grail chapel at Whittington.

ABOVE. The Grail procession from *La Folie Perceval* (Bibliotheque Nationale).

BELOW. Surviving fragment of Wolfram's original *Parzival* (Bayerische Straatsbibliothwk).

'For thou art my rock and my fortress.' The Red Castle at Hawkstone Park.

'They go down by the valleys.' The White Cliff gorge.

'Lead me to the rock that is higher than I.' White Cliff, as seen from the Red Castle.'

ABOVE. 'Thou art my hiding place.' The Grotto at Hawkstone Park where the chalice was discovered.'

LEFT. 'I looked on my right hand and beheld.' The window of the four Evangelists in Hodnet church.

'Ye that stand in the house of the Lord.' Hodnet parish church.

ABOVE and OPPOSITE. The trumps from the Marseilles Tarot pack – the key to the mystery of the Holy Grail.

LA ROUE DE FORTUNE

LA FORCE

LE PENDU

LA MORT

TEMPERANCE

LA MAISON DE DIEU

LE SOLEIL

LE IUGEMENT

LE MONDE

The historical Excalibur, re-created by Wilkinson Sword.

The cup discovered at Hawkstone Park. Is this the Marian Chalice – the historical Grail?

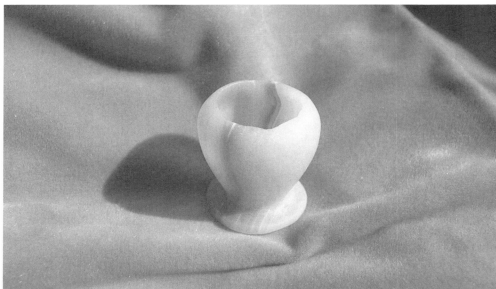

century Welsh; Blayse lived in the early twelfth century and came from St Asaph in north Wales. As Blayse is also accredited with the story that inspired the *Didcot Perceval*, the two were most likely the same. In other words, the *Peveril* poem was the original Grail romance.

Unfortunately, the author of the *Fulke* romance only included brief passages from the *Peveril* in his narrative, so we know frustratingly little about Payne Peveril's life. What we do know for certain is that his wife Lynette was the direct descendant of Owain Ddantgwyn (see Chapter VIII), and therefore a member of the family who may have been the guardians of the Marian Chalice – the historical Grail.

In *Fulke le Fitz Waryn* the Grail is discovered by Payne Peveril's great-grandson Fulk, who lived around a century later. After travelling halfway around Europe, Fulk eventually returns home to discover the Grail in the vaults of his own chapel in Whittington:

> And there in the chapel of St Augustine that is fair did Fulk look
> upon the Grail, which Our Lord and Saviour did give into the hands
> of his servant Joseph.

This chapel was an actual building destroyed after the dissolution of the monasteries in the mid sixteenth century. The ruins of Whittington Castle still survive, and the chapel site is now a scenic garden just outside the castle walls. From the records of Shrewsbury Abbey we know that the chapel was built around 1090 with an endowment from Payne Peveril himself.

Nearly all the Grail romances house the Grail in a chapel attached to the Grail castle. Perhaps the chapel at Whittington was the true Grail chapel. Perhaps, as Arthur's direct living heir, Payne's wife Lynette had requested the chapel built to house the Marian Chalice.

The chalice, however, is not the only Grail in *Fulke le Fitz Waryn*. As in other romances, there is more than one Grail involved – a second relic, a book, is also described as the Grail. In the *Peveril* section of the *Fulke* romance we are told that a man must learn to balance his wisdom and his power if he is to achieve enlightenment. The verse goes on to say: 'This the Grail tells us, the book of the holy vessel'. As the words 'holy vessel' seem here to be describing Christ rather than the cup, like the book referenced in the Vulgate romance (see Chapter V) this Grail seems to be a secret text containing words spoken by Jesus himself. If the Grail romances were orginally allegories concerning an alternative apostolic succession from Joseph of Arimathea (see Chapter V), then this 'book of the holy vessel' might have been an alternative gospel. If such a book really did exist the threat to the teachings of the established Church would have been enormous. Unfortunately, *Fulke le Fitz Waryn* makes no further mention of the book.

Fulke le Fitz Waryn only contains extracts from the lost *Peveril*. However, the original may have directly inspired a fourteenth-century French romance. Known as *La Folie Perceval*, it may contain the most complete translation of the *Peveril* poem still to survive.

Summary

- Although much within the Grail romance is clearly fictitious, like Arthur, there may have been an historical character upon whom the legendary Perceval was based. A passage in the *Didcot Perceval* contains a vital clue that ultimately leads us to just such a figure. According to the *Didcot Perceval*, the original Grail story was taken from 'a book in the British language, which was dictated to Brother Blayse'. A number of modern literary scholars have proposed the author to be a monk with the same name, recorded at the abbey of St Asaph in north Wales in the late eleventh century.

- The author of the *Didcot Perceval* makes Blayse Perceval's contemporary. However, Blayse the St Asaph monk lived some six centuries after the historical Arthurian period. It is possible, therefore, that the medieval Grail story originated with two separate traditions, one holding that Perceval's family were the true Grail guardians, the other that this honour belonged to the family of Arthur. In reality, the historical Perceval may have been descendant of the historical Arthur who lived during Blayse's time.

- *Fulke le Fitz Waryn* contains what appear to be extracts from the oldest Grail romance, the *Peveril*. Here the historical Payne Peveril – a contemporary of Blayse – is the Grail hero. In the story Payne Peveril bears remarkable similarities to Perceval in the Grail romance. Not only is his name – Peveril – similar to Perceval, but he was the son of an Alan le Crux. In the *Didcot Perceval* Perceval's father is called Alain li Gros. Payne Peveril's castle is called 'the White Castle', the name applied to Perceval's Grail castle in *Perlesvaus*. According to the *Fulke* romance Payne Peveril's castle had once belonged to someone named Bran, and nearly all the Grail romances give the Fisher King a very similar name – Bron. Three of the romances place the Grail castle in or near 'the White Town', and Payne Peveril's castle was in the White Town of Whittington. Accordingly, Payne Peveril may have been the historical Perceval, upon whom later, more fanciful tales were based.

- Blayse was almost certainly the author of the *Peveril* – the original Grail romance. Not only was he Payne Peveril's contemporary, he became his personal chaplain in 1090. Furthermore, the *Peveril* was written in early-twelfth-century Welsh; Blayse lived in the early twelfth century and came from St Asaph in north Wales.

- In *Fulke le Fitz Waryn* the Grail is housed in a chapel attached to Whittington Castle. Payne Peveril's wife Lynette was the direct descendant of Owain Ddantgwyn. Accordingly, she may have genuinely possessed the historical Grail – the Marian Chalice – which she had placed in the chapel that once stood beside Whittington Castle.

Chapter XI

Perceval the Fool

La Folie Perceval now survives in a manuscript preserved in the Bibliothèque Nationale, Paris. Catalogued as *MS Fonds français 12577*, the manuscript itself dates from around 1330 and contains a number of Arthurian tales copied by the same anonymous scribe. As other stories in the manuscript are prose versions of earlier Arthurian poems, such as Wace's *Roman de Brut* and Chretien's *Lancelot*, it seems that the scribe was attempting to translate into prose all the early Arthurian romances. The sources for the other works still survive in earlier copies, although an original *Folie* has not yet been discovered. The reason for believing that it may have been based on the same romance as the *Peveril* sections in *Fulke le Fitz Waryn*, however, is that the opening lines of both are almost identical.

The *Peveril* section of *Fulke le Fitz Waryn* opens with Merlin's prediction concerning the coming of a great warrior:

> The leopard will follow the wolf,
> And with his tail will threaten him.
> The wolf will leave the woods and mounts,
> Will remain in the water with the fishes,
> And will pass over the sea,
> Will encircle the whole island.
> At last he will conquer the leopard
> By his cunning and by his art;
> Then he will come into this land
> Will have his stronghold in the water.

The *Folie* begins with virtually the same prophecy:

94

The leopard will follow the wolf, and will threaten him with his tail and drive him into the sea. But the wolf will return from the sea to conquer the leopard by stealth and by cunning. Then he will come to the White Land and build his castle on an island in a lake.

In *Fulke le Fitz Waryn* the passage is seen as a prophecy concerning Fulk's quarrel with King John, and his ultimate possession of Whittingon Castle. In the *Folie* the same prophesy is said to refer to Perceval's quarrel with a Red Knight, and his eventual building of a new Grail castle in the White Town.

The inclusion of the same prophecy suggests a shared source of both romances, namely the original *Peveril*. But whereas *Fulke le Fitz Waryn* contains only a few verses from the poem, the *Folie* seems to continue with the full story. Although the hero in the romance is Perceval and not Payne Peveril, the two share many similarities. For example, Peveril built the castle at Whittington, the historical White Town, and it was constructed on a lake island in the Great Marche, just as Perceval's is. The author of the *Folie* may simply have changed the name from Peveril to Perceval as, by the time he was writing, in the fourteenth century, the Arthurian knight had become inseparably linked with the Grail story. We have already seen how other authors altered the name, such as Parzival in Wolfram's version, and Peredur in the Welsh.

Further indication that the *Folie* is based on the *Peveril* concerns the description of one of the Grails as a book. Like the *Peveril* section in *Fulke*, the *Folie* describes it as 'the book of the holy vessel'. No other surviving romance uses this precise description.

It seems likely that the *Folie* is a fairly accurate rendering of the original poem, since none of the other stories contained in the manuscript have been elaborated by the copyist, merely translated into prose. Accordingly, it may be a close rendition to the first medieval Grail romance.

The literal translation of *La Folie Perceval* is 'The Mad Perceval'. However, a more accurate interpretation is 'Perceval the Fool'. In the story, the foolish and naive young man must learn to become wise in the ways of the world before he can take his rightful place as the guardian of the Grail. Following Merlin's prophecy, the *Folie* continues with Perceval's encounter with a mysterious Red Knight. The knight tells Perceval that he must defeat him in combat if he is to pass over a bridge he is guarding, a theme that occurs in many later Arthurian romances,

95

although the protagonists are then portrayed as Arthur and Lancelot. Although he fights bravely, Perceval is beaten. The knight, however, agrees to spare Perceval's life for one year, in which time he must acquire the skills to defeat his opponent or die. Once again, this theme occurs in a later romance, *Sir Gawain and the Green Knight* (*circa* 1400), in which the Green Knight offers the same bargain to Gawain.

After the knight leaves, Perceval is met by Merlin, who tells him that the only way to better the Red Knight is by seeking the wisdom of the Grail. At this point we are not told what the Grail actually is, or precisely what wisdom it might reveal. Merlin returns to the forest and Perceval sets out to find the Grail castle. Before long he meets a wise woman beside the road who tells him the whereabouts of the castle, 'the castle of the Fisher King in the Old Marche'. Once again the castle is in the Old Marche, the name for the Welsh borderland around Whittington, just as it is described in *Fulke le Fitz Waryn* and the *Didcot Perceval*.

When Perceval eventually finds the castle he is invited to a banquet held in honour of the Fisher King and his wife the Queen. During the feast a procession enters from a side chapel bearing 'the Grail Hallows'. The *Folie* manuscript includes an illustration of the procession showing a maiden carrying a chalice, followed by a page with a lance, and four servants bearing a draped box with a sword on top. Later in the story we are told the significance of the Grail Hallows: the holy chalice contained Christ's blood, the lance pierced his side during the Crucifixion, the sword beheaded John the Baptist, and the draped box holds the plate of the Last Supper. The servants place the box before the King and Queen and open it to reveal the sacred platter:

> And upon the platter was the book of the holy vessel, but Perceval could not look upon it for it shone with so great a light.

The King, however, is unaffected by the light and is able to read from the book. Again we find a link with the *Peveril* section in *Fulke le Fitz Waryn*, for the King tells Perceval that he must balance both power and wisdom if he is to make a wise king. Perceval is amazed at the spectacle, and mystified as to why the Fisher King should give him such advice but, as in the other Grail romances, he fails to question his host. The banquet then ends and the Fisher King retires alone to the Grail chapel where he intends to spend the night at prayer.

Later, Perceval decides to follow the King into the chapel, in the hope of seeing the Grail Hallows once more. Inside, he finds the King gone, and is confronted instead by a hooded man whom he assumes to be a priest. The man tells him that he must leave the castle as he has failed to ask about what he has seen and heard. Perceval is temporarily blinded by a brilliant flash of light, and when he recovers his sight he finds himself standing in the forest accompanied by the wise woman.

The story follows the same theme as the other romances when the wise woman tells Perceval that the Fisher King is his grandfather. However, it most closely corresponds to the *Peveril* in that the name of the Fisher King is Bran. The woman explains that Bran is the guardian of the Grail Hallows, and that he cannot die until he has been replaced by a successor. Like the other Grail romances, Perceval is that successor, although he cannot become the new Fisher King until he has asked the right question. The book, we are told, contains the secret words spoken by Christ himself, and only the Fisher King can read from it. When Perceval asks the woman how she knows these things, she explains:

'I was once as he who sent you here. I am the eagle who flew higher than any who dwelt in Rome. It is I who drank the wine of Peter and Joseph both.'

With this mysterious riddle, the wise woman vanishes into the forest.

Throughout the main body of the story Perceval experiences a series of adventures while searching for the Grail castle. He encounters a number of strange characters, each of whom sets him tasks to perform or riddles to solve. He meets two lovers sitting beneath a tree who ask him to retrieve a golden apple from a giant, a charioteer who holds a bleeding spear that seems to be one of the Grail Hallows, a hermit who reveals to him a vision of the Crucifixion, and a cowled figure who kills the grass over which he walks.

Eventually Perceval finds the Grail castle, which has been reduced to ruins by a lightning bolt cast down by the devil. Unable to die, the Fisher King is now alone amongst the rubble. Although frail and weak, he invites Perceval to dine with him. This time it is no banquet but a simple meal of bread and wine. When the Fisher King breaks the bread to share it with his guest, the Grail procession again enters the hall. This time as the sacred book is opened Perceval asks the right question: 'Whom does the Grail serve?' Satisfied that the conditions have been met for Perceval to take over his role, the King hands him the book, answering: 'The Grail serves the Fisher King.' Although it still shines brightly, Perceval can now read the text.

Unlike in the other Grail romances, where the significance of this strange question remains a mystery, the *Folie* makes it quite plain. When the King offers Perceval the book, telling him that 'this Grail' serves the Fisher King' it clearly shows that Perceval has proved himself worthy to become the new Fisher King. Moreover, the book itself seems to be *the* Grail, as Perceval is told that it serves the Fisher King while he hands it over.

The old King then teaches Perceval about the book, and how it contains the secret words of Jesus written down by Didymus, a disciple of Christ. He is also told about the characters he has met during his quest. The man whom he took to be a priest was in fact the Pope, the lovers were Adam and Eve, the hermit was Joseph of Arimathea, the charioteer was the Roman soldier who pierced the side of Christ, and the cowled figure was the Grim Reaper, death itself.

When the Fisher King has finished explaining, an angel appears to take him to heaven. It is then that the Red Knight returns to tell Perceval that his year is up, and he must fight for his honour. Perceval accepts the challenge, but is again defeated. The Red Knight runs him through with his sword but, as the new Fisher King, Perceval cannot die and immediately recovers. The Red Knight then laughs and announces that honour is satisfied. He removes his helmet to reveal that he is really Merlin. He set the year-long quest for Perceval so that he could learn to become a worthy Fisher King. The story ends with Perceval building a new Grail castle, 'the White Castle of the White Town', and a 'white maiden' taking the sacred book 'into another place', presumably heaven.

There can be little doubt that the *Folie* is an allegory concerning an apostolic succession. Just before his life on earth is over, the Fisher King invites Perceval to a simple meal of bread and wine, just as Jesus did with the disciples at the Last Supper. The Fisher King has taken the place of Christ, and like Christ he ascends bodily into heaven. Perceval then replaces him as Peter does Jesus. The fact that during Perceval's first visit the Pope himself is the only person in the chapel in which the Fisher King should have been praying surely symbolises that the Fisher King is himself the Pope. In other words, he is of the true apostolic line. Again Joseph of Arimathea appears in the story to impart a vision of the

Crucifixion, presumably signifying that the succession is from Joseph and not from Peter, as taught by the established Church.

As we have seen, the source of the *Folie* is almost certainly the same source as the *Peveril* in the *Fulke* romance. However, was this source really the oldest Grail romance – the original upon which Chrétien and his contemporaries based their versions of the story? The surviving copy of the *Folie* only dates from the 1330s, and so was transcribed almost a century and a half after the early romances. The general consensus amongst literary historians is that the *Folie* is a late romance, a compilation from the original eight. As the fifteenth-century Thomas Malory compiled his *Le Morte d'Arthur* from all the famous Arthurian romances available at the time, so the author of the *Folie* did likewise with the Grail stories. It is argued that even if the writer of the extant manuscript did adhere strictly to the story he was transcribing into prose, the story itself was already a much later romance than those of Chrétien and his contemporaries.

Conversely, the *Folie* does have a feeling of authenticity about it. Whereas the allegorical significance and symbolism of the other romances remains vague and unclear, in the *Folie* it is far more apparent. Not only is the meaning of the final meal and Perceval's question more obvious, but the significance of the Grail is easier to understand. In all the romances the Grail seems to impart some special wisdom, but precisely how it does this is always obscure. For example: in the First Continuation the Grail is an unnamed floating object that somehow satiates a thirst for knowledge; the *Perlesvaus* Grail is a nebulous artefact in which visions somehow appear; while Chrétien de Troyes fails to explain how his Grail works. We get the impression that the authors did not fully understand the significance of their material. The *Folie* author, however, leaves his reader with no doubt as to how his Grail discloses wisdom – it is a book containing secret words spoken by Christ. Although the Vulgate version does include as one of its Grails a book written by Jesus himself, this plays almost no part in the story. Indeed, the Grail seen during the banquet is the cup of the Last Supper.

Alternatively, the *Folie* author may appear more conversant with his subject matter simply because it was written much later. By the fourteenth century, the time of the extant copy, the Grail romances had been in circulation long enough for any imaginative writer to inject convincing interpretations of the symbolism into the existing story. All the same, the similarities with the *Perevil* sections of *Fulke le Fitz Waryn* still remain, and that seems to have been a poem written almost a century before Chrétien and his contemporaries composed their works.

A similar either-way argument can be made concerning the characters in the saga. The figures that Perceval encounters during his quest to find the Grail castle in the *Folie* appear scattered though the other Grail romances. For example: the hermit is included in some, and the wise woman in others; the lovers appear in the *Didcot Perceval*, the charioteer features in the First Continuation, and the Grim Reaper is found in the Vulgate Cycle. This could either imply that the traditional romancers only had fragmentary knowledge of an earlier story upon which the *Folie* was based, or that the *Folie* author attempted to construct a complete story from all the others. Which is correct? If the hermit, the wise woman, the lovers, the Reaper, and the charioteer truly belong in the same story, then it would greatly strengthen the case for the *Folie* being the earliest of the Grail romances.

Each time I studied the *Folie* I had the distinct impression that these strange characters *did* belong together; I was sure I had come across them somewhere before. It was some time before I finally realised where – in the Tarot pack.

The oldest known Tarot pack dates from the mid fifteenth century. Although the origins of the Tarot are obscure, there are references to the cards in the writing of a Swiss monk almost a hundred years earlier, in 1377. By the late sixteenth century they were being widely used as gaming cards all over Europe. Although today there are many different Tarot designs, the original cards, such as the French Marseilles pack dating from around 1500, consisted of four suits of fourteen cards, and a set of twenty-two named cards called the trumps. The four suits were similar to modern playing cards – which probably derived from the Tarot – but instead of spades, hearts, diamonds and clubs, they included swords, cups, coins and staffs. Each suit is similar to modern playing cards in that they are numbered from ace to ten, but they have four court cards instead of three: a page, a knight, a queen and a king. At some point during their development into modern playing cards the page became a jack and the knight was dropped. The twenty-two trump cards were also abandoned. It is on these trump cards of the Tarot that the characters from the *Folie* appear. The trumps consisted of a series of strange medieval figures and symbols, all but one, the Fool, having a number:

Perceval the Fool

Number and Name	Brief Description
– The Fool	A journeying jester with a dog
1. The Magician	A conjuror performing before a table
2. The Female Pope	A woman wearing a papal crown
3. The Emperor	An enthroned man holding a sceptre
4. The Empress	A woman holding a shield and sceptre
5. The Pope	A pope with two attendants
6. The Lovers	A man, two women and a cupid
7. The Charioteer	A youth driving a two-horse chariot
8. Justice	A female holding a sword and scales
9. The Hermit	An old man with a staff and lantern
10. The Wheel of Fortune	Three strange beasts on a spit wheel
11. Strength	A woman holding closed a lion's jaws
12. The Hanged Man	A tied figure hanging upside down
13. Death	A skeleton with a scythe
14. Temperance	A winged woman with two goblets
15. The Devil	The Devil with two bound imps
16. The Falling Tower	A tower struck by lightning
17. The Star	A naked woman under a star-filled sky
18. The Moon	Two dogs howling at the full moon
19. The Sun	The sun shining down on two children
20. Judgement	An angel summoning the dead to rise
21. The World	A bull, lion, eagle, angel, and maiden

Five of these characters – the Hermit, the Lovers, the Charioteer, Death, and the Pope – feature in the _Folie_; even the magician is present in the form of Merlin. Moreover, they even appear in numberical order. Perceval is advised by Merlin the magician to search for the Grail, and he later meets a pope, the lovers, and the charioteer in immediate succession. In the Tarot the Magician is number 1, the Pope is 5, the Lovers 6, and the Charioteer 7. Both the hermit and the Reaper apear later in the story; in the Tarot the Hermit is number 9 and Death is 13.

Did any of the other cards feature in the romance? The first character Perceval encounters after Merlin sets him on his quest is a wise woman – the Female Pope perhaps? He next meets the king and the queen of the Grail Castle – the Emperor and the Empress? Some of the other cards could also be present. The Falling Tower and the Devil might be related to the devil destroying the Grail castle with a lightning bolt. The

101

Judgement card might pertain to the Fisher King's ascension into heaven, and Perceval's inheritance of the sacred book might correlate with the final card, the World. This card shows an angel, a lion, a bull and an eagle, all surrounding a naked woman. Since early Christian times these four creatures have been used to symbolise the four gospels, Matthew, Mark, Luke and John. In the *Folie* the Grail is the book of Jesus' teachings written by the disciple Didymus – a fifth gospel. The book is eventually taken away by a mysterious maiden, possibly the naked woman of the World card. Finally, the unnumbered Fool card, showing a jester journeying with a pack on his back, might relate to Perceval himself, the naive quest hero who ultimately attains enlightenment.

Even the suit cards might be linked with the story. There is a king, a queen, a knight and a page in the *Folie*. Moreover, the symbols for the four suits are remarkably similar to the four Grail Hallows: the sword, the chalice, the lance and the platter. The sword and the chalice are present in the suits of swords and cups, and a lance is similar to a staff. The suit usually described as coins, or sometimes pentacles, is represented by a circular disc, possibly a plate.

I was convinced that there was some relationship between the *Folie* and the Tarot – the question was what. Initially I needed to discover which came first. Was the Tarot a pictorial representation of the Grail romance, or was the Grail romance a literary rendition of the Tarot?

Summary

- *La Folie Perceval* (surviving in a manuscript dating from around 1330) seems to have been a translation into prose of the *Peveril* sections in *Fulke le Fitz Waryn*, as a number of verses are almost identical. Although the hero in the romance is Perceval and not Payne Peveril, the two share many similarities. For example, Peveril built the castle at Whittington, the historical White Town, and it was built on a lake island in the Great Marche, just as Perceval's is. The author of the *Folie* may simple have changed the name from Peveril to Perceval as, by the time he was writing in the fourteenth century, the Arthurian knight had become inseparably limked with the Grail story. As in the *Fulke* romance, the *Folie* also describes the Grail as 'the book of the holy vessel'.

• Throughout the main body of the *Folie*, Perceval experiences a series of adventures while searching for the Grail Castle. He encounters a number of strange characters, such as the Pope, two lovers, a hermit, a charioteer, and the Grim Reaper, death, each of whom sets him tasks to perform or riddles to solve. In the Grail castle Perceval witnesses a procession bearing 'the Grail Hallows': a sword, a lance, a plate and a cup. The most holly relic, however, is a book – seemingly the Grail itself – which can only be read by the Fisher King. We are told that the book contains the secret words of Jesus written down by his disciple Didymus.

• Remarkably, the *Folie* seems to be a literary rendition of the Tarot pack. The origins of the Tarot are obscure, but they are recorded from as early as the fourteenth century. The pack consists of four suits of fourteen cards, and a set of twenty-two named cards called the trumps. The four suits are swords, cups, coins and staffs. Each suit is numbered from ace to ten and has four court cards: a page, a knight, a queen and a king.

• In the twenty-two trump cards of the Tarot a number of the characters from the *Folie* appear – the Hermit, the Lovers, the Charioteer, Death and the Pope, and the Magician. Perceval's inheritance of the sacred book might correlate with the final card, the World. This card shows an angel, a lion, a bull and an eagle, all surrounding a naked woman. Since early Christian times these four creatures have been used to symbolise the four gospels, Matthew, Mark, Luke and John. In the *Folie* the Grail is a book of Jesus' secret teachings – a fifth gospel. Finally, the unnumbered Fool card might relate to Perceval himself. It will be remembered that the title of the romance, *La Folie Perceval*, actually translates as 'Perceval the Fool'.

• Even the suit cards of the Tarot appear to be linked with the story. There is a king, a queen, a knight and a page in the *Folie*. Moreover, the symbols for the four suits are remarkably similar to the four Grail Hallows: the sword, the chalice, the lance and the platter. The sword and the chalice are present in the suits of swords and cups, and a lance is similar to a staff. The suit usually described as coins, or sometimes pentacles, is represented by a circular disc, possibly a plate.

Chapter XII

The Mystery of the Tarot

The popular belief that Tarot cards arrived with the gypsies is historically unfounded. Originating in north-west India, these nomadic people migrated westwards into Europe during the sixteenth century. (The name gypsy stemmed from the erroneous belief that they came from Egypt.) The Tarot, however, was already in circulation in Europe at least a hundred years earlier.

There still survive a number of Tarot packs which pre-date the arrival of the gypsies, the oldest being seventeen cards from an Italian deck preserved in the Bibliothèque Nationale in Paris, dating from about 1470. The Visconti pack from Spain dates from around 1480, and the Marseilles pack from France was made shortly after. The fact that they were so widely dispersed over half a century before the gypsies arrived clearly shows that the Tarot was here first. Although the gypsies eventually became famous for their fortune-telling, they seem merely to have adopted the Tarot for the purpose. Indeed, it seems highly unlikely that the Tarot originated anywhere outside Europe, as the characters the cards portray, such as the Pope, the Devil, and the evangelical symbols on the World card, are purely Christian in concept.

The earliest recorded purchase of cards is found in the ledgers of the dukedom of Brabant in 1379, and in 1392 the court treasurer to Charles VI of France records payment for the artist Gringonneur to paint a private pack. Other records of the Tarot are found in legislation that either banned or permitted the cards' use for gaming purposes. In Regensburg in Germany they were banned in 1378, whereas they were permitted by a decree in Nuremberg in 1380, and were listed amongst the allowed games of Florence in 1393. These historical references demonstrate how widespread the cards had become by the end of the fourteenth century. This means that they were probably first introduced some time in the mid 1300s. As the manuscript containing *La Folie Perceval* was written around 1330, the Tarot and the romance appear to date from approximately the same period.

As the *Folie* romance was virtually unknown in fourteenth-century Europe (the romances of Chrétien and his contemporaries were the popular stories), it seems unlikely that the Tarot would have been a game based around it. The other possibility is that someone decided to base a romance on the Tarot. However, as we have seen, the *Folie* seems to have been taken from a Welsh poem written around 1100. If there is a connection between the Tarot and the *Folie* – which there certainly seems to be – then some concept must have existed which inspired both.

Although the Tarot was widely used from the fifteenth century as a gaming pack, and more recently evolved into the popular playing cards, there have been many theories that it originally served a very different purpose. Over the years a number of scholars have proposed that the Tarot may hold religious or mystical significance.

In 1781 the French historian Antoine de Gebelin wrote *Le Jeu De Tarots*, in which he suggested that the Tarot contained occult symbolism from ancient Egypt. He proposed that the cards had originally been based on an Egyptian magical text called *The Book of Thoth*. The trump cards, he believed, had once depicted Egyptian gods and guardians of the underworld. Although de Gebelin's theory attracted a considerable following at the time, it was eventually discredited when the Rosetta Stone was discovered in 1799. A basalt slab containing inscriptions from the second century BC, the Rosetta Stone became the key to deciphering Egyptain hierogliphics. It was soon shown that Egyptian mythology and *The Book of Thoth* bore little or no relationship to the symbolism of the Tarot pack.

One of de Gebelin's associates, Alliette, a Parisian antiquarian, published his own work on the Tarot in 1783. He also believed that the Tarot orginally held important occult significance. However, his theory differed from de Gebelin's in that he believed that the cards had originally been used for fortune-telling. Before long, Alleitte, or Etteilla as he later called himself, became the most famous fortune-teller in France. Thereafter, Tarot cards became popular for fortune-telling all over Europe, and were adopted by the gypsies some time in the early nineteenth century. The debate concerning the Tarot as ancient occult pictograms, or as a system of divination had thus begun.

In the mid nineteenth century the occultist Alphonse Constant, better known as Eliphas Levi, published a number of works on magic and occultism. Having studied theology, Levi believed that the Tarot trumps were associated with a mystical Hebrew system known as the Cabbala. Also called 'The Tree of Life', the Cabbala first appeared with a Jewish sect in twelfth-century Spain. In essence, the system concerned a pictorial design divided into a number of circles connected by a series of lines, or paths. Each circle (or Sefiroth) represented a different level of consciousness, while the paths represented the relationships between them. Although it has often been proposed that the Cabbala dated back to Biblical times, and was originally a secret, inner doctrine taught by Moses, there is no surviving historical evidence to date it earlier than the 1100s.

In the Cabbala, each of the twenty-two paths corresponded with a letter from the Hebrew alphabet, and Levi believed that the twenty-two Tarot trumps originally served a similar role. The symbolism of each card, he proposed, represented the path and the mystical experience involved in achieving the various levels of consciousness. He also linked the four suits with the four elements, earth, air, fire and water, and considered the entire pack to be the key to understanding ancient magic. Another occultist, Oswald Wirth, designed a pack of cards based on these ideas, although Levi's greatest exponent was an occultist who went by the name of Papus. In his *Tarot of the Bohemians*, published in the 1890s, he integrated Wirth's cards with Levi's theories to add a new dimension of Cabbalistic meaning to the Tarot.

Another school of thought which originated in England in the late nineteenth century came from the occult society, the Order of the Golden Dawn. The Golden Dawn followed Levi's lead by adopting the Cabbalistic concept of the Tarot, although they took the whole notion much further. The man largely responsible for this development was Samuel Mathers, later known as McGregor Mathers, who also incorporated the zodiac signs and the planets into the scheme. By this time new mystical names were also given to the trumps and suits of the Tarot – the major and minor arcana, from the word 'arcane', meaning secret knowledge. The ideas of Mathers and the Golden Dawn inspired a redesigned Tarot pack which included elaborate symbolic pictures on all of the fifty-six suit cards as well as the twenty-two trumps. Designed by Golden Dawn member A. E. Waite, and painted by the artist Pamela Coleman Smith, the pack first appeared in print in 1916. Having significantly influenced many subsequent Tarot designs, it is now called the Rider/Waite pack, and is probably the most popular Tarot deck in the world today.

We can see, therefore, that any magical associations with the Tarot are late developments. If there really was some mystical meaning to the Tarot it is more likely to be Christian than occult. The view of most modern historians is that the Tarot probably orginated with the Albigenses, an heretical Christian sect who flourished around Toulouse in southern France between the eleventh and thirteenth centuries. (The word Albigenses comes from their stronghold town of Albi.) The Albigenses believed in the duality of good and evil, and envisaged Jesus as having rebelled against the cruelty of un uncaring God who had left the world to the whims of the devil.

Many surviving Albigensian texts show the cup of the Eucharist in exactly the same unique style as the cups drawn on the original Tarot decks, which have a symbol of four leaves descending from the bowl. Unknown outside Albigensian symbolism, it represented the Trinity with the added respect of the devil – or demi-urge – the imagined ruler of the earth in Albigensian philosophy.

The sect was subjected to the most appalling persecutions. From 1209 they were hunted down by an army appointed by Pope Innocent III, to be followed by wholesale and indiscriminate massacres initiated by the French king Louis VIII in 1219. By the time the atrocities ended, two and a half decades later, thousands had been killed. It is suggested that the Tarot cards were originally a pictorial book of Albigensian teachings, secretly concealed as gaming cards to avoid discovery by their persecutors. More likely, they had been a mnemonic device, a kind of mental shorthand, just as many students today use visual memory tricks to help retain key facts for examinations. The thirteenth-century theologian Thomas Aquinas refers to such cards being used in southern France shortly after the Albigensian persecutions had ended. He calls them the *Ars Notoria*, but unfortunately neglects to describe them.

The most telling clue to link the Tarot cards with the Albigenses is the Tarot trump the Female Pope. In 1206 Dominic Guzman, the founder of the Catholic Dominican order, began to preach against the Albigenses. He accused them of ordaining women priests and of claiming spiritual descent from a female pope. He refered to her as 'Joanna Aquila' – Joan the Eagle.

In 1245, shortly after the Albigensian persecutions had finally ended, the chronicler Martinus Polonus, who spent time in the area of Toulouse, refered to Pope Joan. He said that she had been a British woman who had travelled with her father to peach the gospel to the Germans during the Dark Ages. She eventually spent time around the monks of the monastery at Fulda, where she became an accomplished scholar. Ultimately, frustrated by the prejudice shown against her as a woman, she decided to leave the area and pose as a man. After journeying to Rome dressed as a friar, she was ordained a priest, and later became a cardinal. According to Martinus:

> [In Rome] she opened a school and acquired such a reputation for learning and feigned sanctity that, on the death of Leo IV, she was made pope. For two years and five months, with the name of John VIII, she filled the papal chair with reputation, no one suspecting her sex. Soon she came with child, some say, from a servant there.
>
> Then at the Rogation, whilst the procession passed before St Clements, she was seized with pains, and fell to the ground amidst the crowd. Whilst her attendants ministered to her she was delivered a son. Some say the mother and child died. Others say that the child was to found the sect of Cathars, or be the Antichrist of the last days.

The Cathars was another name by which the Albigenses were known, and the reference to the Antichrist shows quite clearly how they were perceived by Catholics. The Church authorities vehemently denied the story of Pope Joan. However, two centuries before Martinus, around 1060, the Cologne monk Marianus Scotus wrote in his chronicle:

> Lotharii 14 [in the fourteenth year of the Holy Roman Emperor Lothair I], Joanna, a woman, succeeded Leo, and reigned two years, five months and two days.

The fourteenth year of Lothair's reign was 854. If John VIII was really Joan, as Martinus asserts, then this dating is historically inaccurate. Pope Leo IV reigned from 847 to 855, and was immediately succeeded by Pope Benedict III. There was, however, an historical Pope John VIII, who *was* suspected of being a woman. Around 1100 another chronicler, Sigebert of Gemblours, wrote of John VIII, saying: 'It is reported that this John was a female.' This pope, who reigned from 872 to 882, did die under mysterious circumstances, murdered by a group of Italian nobles, seemingly under orders from the Holy Roman Emperor Charles III. Indeed, something very unusual seems to have been discovered about John VIII, as the entire papal electoral procedure was immediately changed after his death. Perhaps the Church intended to make certain they were never duped again?

It is with the story of the female pope that we find the most compelling evidence to link the Tarot with *La Folie Perceval*. Perceval is with the Pope in the Grail chapel before he is mysteriously transported back to the forest to find himself accompanied by the wise woman. After she reveals his lineage, the woman explains how she is so knowledgeable: 'I was once as he who sent you here.' As it was the pope figure who seems to have transported Perceval from the Grail castle to the wise woman's forest, she appears to be saying that she too was a pope. Her next line is even more significant: 'I am the eagle who flew higher than any who dwelt in Rome.' According to Dominic Guzman in 1206, the female pope was called 'Joanna Aquila', Joan the Eagle, and as pope she *would* have ranked higher than anyone in the Roman Catholic Church. This clearly shows that not only is the wise woman of the *Folie* the Female Pope of the Tarot pack, but she is also perceived as Pope Joan.

For the Tarot to be linked so closely with the *Folie* and the Albigenses, there must be a connection between the Grail romances and this strange religious sect. If the Tarot did contain the coded teachings of the Albigenses, then presumably the *Folie* was another version of the same system. The Albigenses first appeared around 1100, and the *Folie*, in the form of the *Peveril*, seems also to date from about that time. However, the Grail romances concerned a British blood line, whereas the Albigenses can be traced back to their eleventh-century forerunners, the Bogomils of the Balkans. As there seems no medieval connection between the two, they must both have inherited the Tarot symbolism from some earlier source.

The central mystery of the Grail romances seems to have been an alternative apostolic succession; the Albigenses claimed something similar. They believed that they had the right to perform mass because their priests were ordained by priests with a line returning to Pope Joan. Here we have a direct cross-reference with the Grail romance. In the *Folie* the wise woman tells Perceval: 'It is I who drank the wine of Peter and Joseph both.' As the papess, she is of Catholic apostolic succession from Peter, although she is also of the line of Jospeh of Arimathea. Here, the Female Pope – who we have already established must be Pope Joan –

is clearly portrayed as a member of the Grail family. Indeed, whenever the wise woman appears in the other romances, she is always portrayed as Perceval's relative. It seems that both the Albigenses and the historical Grail family were claiming descent from the same person. So who was this mysterious Pope Joan?

Marianus Scotus tells us that she became pope in 854, but this was eighteen years before the historical John VIII became pope. The date, however, may have concerned her arrival in Rome. If so, we discover a remarkable coincidence. This is precisely the year that according to the *Welsh Annals* Cyngen, the direct descendant of Owain Ddantgwyn – and possibly an historical Grail guardian – travelled to Rome to dispute the claim of Holy Roman Emperor (see Chapter VIII). If Pope Joan really was a member of the historical Grail family, as the *Folie* implies, then she must have been a close relative of Cyngen, perhaps his daughter. Martinus actually says that Joan was British and that she initially travelled to the Continent with her father. The Welsh genealogies show that when Cyngen died he was succeeded via his sister Nest, so he obviously left no child in Britian. Perhaps Joan, the true heir, had chosen to enter the Church, be ordained a priest and thus join the two apostolic lines. Although this is mere speculation, the fact remains that in the early Middle Ages both the Albigenses and the initiators of the Grail romances seem to have held very similar beliefs.

Unlike the historical Grail family, enough has survived concerning Albigensian belief to know precisely where it originated – with an early Christian esoteric cult called the Gnostics. The Gnostics flourished in Alexandria, in Egypt, as early as the second century. Like the Albigenses, they believed in the duality of good and evil – Christ and the demi-urge. However, they rejected the redemption of the Resurrection, believing instead that the demi-urge created the body to imprison the soul. This could only be set free through knowledge and enlightenment as taught by secret words of Jesus. After the Roman Empire adopted Christianity as the State Religion, the Gnostics were considered heretics and progressively forced underground to become secret societies, such as the Bogomils from whom the Albigenses were descended. Consequently, if the Tarot contained Albigensian teachings, then they must have been Gnostic teachings. The *Folie*, therefore, may also be an enciphered Gnostic text.

A firm connection between the Grail romances and Gnosticism exists in the Gnostic claim to possessing secret words of Jesus. By the time

110

Catholicism was established in the early fourth century, the Church chose to include only four gospels in the Bible: Matthew, Mark, Luke and John. There are known to have existed other supposedly first-hand accounts of Jesus' teachings, such as the Gospel of the Nazarenes, used by the early Church in Jerusalem. Constantine the Great outlawed all such gospels, and ordered copies destroyed. The Gnostics, however, still survived in the more remote areas of the empire, and continued to follow a gospel which they believed contained the inner teachings of Christ. As we have seen, the secret words of Jesus are a central theme in the Grail romances. The *Folie* even has such a book as its Holy Grail – a book containing secret words of Jesus written down by his disciple Didymus.

In the Bible we discover who this Didymus was – the apostle Thomas. In St John, Chapter 20, Verse 4, for instance, we find the disciple referred to as: 'Thomas, one of the twelve, called Didymus'. Remarkably, a Gospel of Thomas not only historically existed, but still survives. Preserved in a series of fourth-century parchments discovered in Egypt in 1945, is a Gnostic gospel which opens:

> These are the words which the living Jesus spoke and Didymus Judas Thomas wrote.

Was this Gospel of Thomas the true Holy Grail?

Summary

- The most telling evidence to link the Tarot cards with the Grail romances is the Tarot trump the Female Pope. The card was derived from the medieval legend that a ninth-century pope had been a woman called Joan the Eagle. In *La Folie Perceval* Perceval meets a wise woman who explains how she was 'once as he who sent you here'. As it was a pope who sent Perceval to the wise woman, she appears to be saying that she too was a pope. Her next line is even more significant: 'I am the eagle who flew higher than any who dwelt in Rome.' Not only was the legendary Pope Joan known as the Eagle, as pope she *would* have ranked higher than anyone in the Roman Catholic Church.

- The view of most modern historians is that the Tarot originated with the Albigenses, an heretical Christian sect who flourished around Toulouse in southern France between the eleventh and thirteenth centuries. Many surviving Albigensian texts show the cup of the Eucharist in exactly the same unique style as the cups drawn on the original Tarot decks, which have a symbol of four leaves descending from the bowl. It is believed that the Tarot cards were originally a pictorial book of Albigensian teachings. The thirteenth-century theologian Thomas Aquinas refers to such cards, calling them the *Ars Notoria*. As the *Folie* seems to have been based on the same symbolism, then the romance must have alluded to a similar philosphy to the Albigenses.

- Albigensian beliefs originated with an early Christian esoteric cult called the Gnostics. Like the Albigenses, they believed that the devil created the body to imprison the soul. This could only be set free through knowledge and enlightenment as taught by secret words of Jesus. Here there exists a firm connection between the Grail romances and Gnosticism. From the earliest Christian times, the Gnostics claimed to follow a gospel containing the inner teachings of Christ, and the secret words of Jesus are a central theme in the Grail romances. The *Folie* even has such a book as its Holy Grail – a book containing secret words of Jesus written down by his disciple Didymus.

- In the Bible, we discover that this Didymus was the apostle Thomas: 'Thomas, one of the twelve, called Didymus'. Remarkably, a Gospel of Thomas still survives. Preserved in a series of fourth-century parchments discovered in Egypt in 1945 is a Gnostic gospel which opens: 'These are the words which the living Jesus spoke and Didymus Judas Thomas wrote.' This Gospel of Thomas may therefore have been the Holy Grail in the original *Folie* Grail romance.

Chapter XIII

The Secret Gospel

In 1945 two Arab farmers were digging for topsoil in a cave in the hills around Nag-Hamadi in Upper Egypt. A few feet below the surface, they uncovered a number of clay pots, containing what they first took to be bundles of worthless card. In fact, they had made as important an historical discovery as the finding of the Dead Sea Scrolls: a volume Gnostic library of texts, dating back to the fourth century AD. It had long been known that the Gnostics of the pre-Catholic era had claimed to have possessed a book of Jesus' teachings omitted from the Bible, but what it contained had remained a complete mystery. Now, after centuries, the world would know: the library included the Gnostic's secret gospel, the Gospel of Thomas.

The Gospel of Thomas was written in Egyptian Coptic, but seems to have been translated from a Greek edition dating back to the mid second century. Its verses matched precisely with a seven-verse fragment found in 1895 and dated from around AD 150. Linguistic analysis of the original seven-verse fragment (known as the *Oxytrhynchus Fragment*) indicated that it had in turn been copied from a first-century document.

Dating from the fourth century, the Gnostic texts had obviously been buried to prevent their destruction by the newly appointed Catholic authorities. The fourth-century cleric Epiphanius lists a number of other such works which were on the Church blacklist, like the Gospel of the Hebrews, the Gospel of the Egyptians, and the Gospel of the Ebionites. Whoever hid the Gospel of Thomas had managed to save the holiest of all Gnostic texts from vanishing forever.

The Gospel of Thomas contains 114 sayings of Jesus, some of which are included in the Biblical Gospels. Most, however, were completely unknown. The Nag-Hamadi discovery caused an uproar in ecclesiastical circles, with many Biblical scholars condemning the Gospel of Thomas as a Gnostic fraud. They pointed out that the Gospel is wholly devoid of detail. It says nothing of the Immaculate Conception, the Crucifixion, or the Resurrection. Even the everyday events surrounding the life of Jesus are absent. In their opinion, this list of teachings had nothing whatsoever to do with the historical Christ. However, its very simplicity might imply the precise opposite.

Before considering this argument, we must first examine the work itself. The full Gospel is too long for the present study, so included below are the opening passages of the text. (The text is printed without chapter or verse numbering, as none were included in the original. Indeed, even the first Bibles had no chapters or verses – they were an addition of the Middle Ages when most books were written in such a fashion.)

These are the secret words which the Living Jesus spoke and Didymus Judas Thomas wrote. And he said: Whoever finds the explanation of these words will not taste death.

Jesus said: Let him who seeks, not cease seeking until he finds, and when he finds, he will be troubled, and when he has been troubled, he will marvel and he will reign over all.

Jesus said: If those who lead you say to you: See, the kingdom is in heaven, then the birds of the heaven will precede you. If they say to you: It is in the sea, then the fish will precede you. But the Kingdom is within you and it is without you. If you will know yourselves, then you will be known and you will know that you are the sons of the living Father. But if you do not know yourselves, then you are in poverty and you are poverty.

Jesus said: The man old in days will not hesitate to ask a little child of seven days about the place of life, and he will live. For many who are first shall become last and shall become a single one.

Jesus said: Know what is in thy sight, and what is hidden from thee will be revealed to thee. For there is nothing hidden which will not be manifest.

His disciples asked him: Wouldst though that we fast and how should we pray and should we give alms, and what diet should we observe? Jesus said: Do not lie; and do not do what you hate, for all things are manifest before Heaven. For there is nothing hidden that shall not be revealed and there is nothing covered that shall remain without being uncovered.

Jesus said: Blessed is the lion which the man eats and the lion will become man; and cursed is the man whom the lion eats and the lion will become man. And He said: The Man is like a wise fisherman who cast his net into the sea, he drew it up and from the sea full of small fish; among them he found a large and good fish, that wise fisherman, he threw all the small fish down into the sea, he chose the large fish without regret. Whoever has ears to hear let him hear.

Jesus said: See, the sower went out, he filled his hand, he threw. Some seeds fell on the road; the birds came, they gathered them. Others fell on the rock and did not strike root in the earth and did not produce ears. And others fell on the thorns; they choked the seed and the worms ate them. And others fell on the good earth; and it brought forth good fruit; it bore sixty per measure and one hundred twenty per measure.

Jesus said: I have cast fire upon the world, and see, I guard it until the world is afire.

Jesus said: This heaven shall pass away and the one above it shall pass away, and the dead are not alive and the living shall not die. In the days when you devoured the dead, you made it alive; when you come into light, what will yo do? On the day when you were one, you became two. But when you have become two, what will you do?

The disciples said to Jesus: We know that thou will go away from us. Who is it who shall be great over us? Jesus said to them: Wherever you have come, you will go to James the righteous for whose sake heaven and earth came into being.

Jesus said to them: If you fast, you will beget sin for yourselves, and if you pray, you will be condemned, and if you give alms, you will do evil to your spirits. And if you go into any land and wander in the regions, if they receive you, eat what they set before you, heal the sick among them. For what goes into your mouth will not defile you.

Jesus said: When you see him who was not born of woman, prostrate yourselves upon your face and adore him: He is your Father.

Jesus said: Men possibly think that I have come to throw peace upon the world and they do not know that I have come to throw division upon the earth, fire, sword and war. For there shall be five in a house: three shall be against two and two against three, the father against the son and the son against the father, and they will stand as solitaries.

Jesus said: I will give you what eye has not seen and what ear has not heard and what hand has not touched and what has not arisen in the heart of man.

The disciples said to Jesus: Tell us how our end will be. Jesus said: Have you then discovered the beginning so that you enquire about the end? For where the beginning is, there shall be the end. Blessed is he who shall stand at the beginning, and he shall know the end and he shall not taste death.

Jesus said: Blessed is he who was before he came into being. If you become disciples to me and hear my words, these stones will minister to you. For you have five trees in Paradise, which are unmoved in summer or in winter and their leaves do not fall. Whoever knows them will not taste death.

The disciples said to Jesus: Tell us what the Kingdom of Heaven is like. He said to them: It is like a mustard seed, smaller than all seeds. But when it falls on the tilled earth, it produces a large branch and becomes shelter for the birds of heaven.

Mary said to Jesus: Whom are thy disciples like? He said: They are like little children who have installed themselves in a field which is not theirs. When the owners of the field come, they will say: Release to us our field. They take off their clothes before them to release the field to them and to give back their field to them. Therefore I say: If the lord of the house knows that the thief is coming, he will stay awake before he comes and will not let him dig through into his house of his kingdom to carry away his goods. You then must watch for the world, gird up your loins with great strength lest the brigands find a way to come to you, because they will find the advantage which you expect. Let there be among you a man of understanding; when the fruit ripened, he came quickly with his sickle in his hand, he reaped it. Whoever has ears to hear let him hear.

Jesus saw children who were being suckled. He said to his disciples: These children who are being suckled are like those who enter the Kingdom. They said to him: Shall we then, being children, enter the Kingdom? Jesus said to them: When you make the two one, and when you make the inner as the outer and the outer as the inner and the above as the below, and when you make the male and the female into a single one, so that the male will not be male and the female not be female, when you make eyes in the place of an eye, and a hand in the place of a hand, and a foot in the place of a foot, and an image in the place of an image, then shall you enter the Kingdom.

Jesus said: I shall choose you, one out of thousand, and two out of ten thousand, and they shall stand as a single one.

His disciples said: Show us the place where Thou art, for it is necessary for us to seek it. He said to them: Whoever has ears let him hear. Within a man of light there is light and he lights the whole world. When he does not shine, there is a darkness.

Jesus said: Love thy brother as thy soul, guard him as the apple of thine eye.

Jesus said: The mote that is in thy brother's eye thou seest, but the beam that is in thine eye, thou seest not. When thou castest the beam out of thine eye, then thou wilt see clearly to cast the mote out of thy brother's eye.

Jesus said: If you fast not from the world, you will not find the Kingdom; if you keep not the Sabbath as Sabbath, you will not see the Father.

Jesus said: I took my stand in the midst of the world and in flesh I appeared to them; found them all drunk, I found none among them athirst. And my soul was afflicted for the sons of men, because they are blind in their heart and do not see that empty they have come into the world and that empty they seek to go out of the world again. But now they are drunk. When they have shaken off their wine, then will they repent.

Jesus said: If the flesh has come into existence because of the spirit, it is a marvel; but if the spirit has come into existence because of the flesh it is a marvel of marvels. But I marvel at the body, at how this great wealth has made its home in this poverty.

Jesus said: Where there are three gods, they are gods; where there are two or one, I am with him.

Jesus said: No prophet is acceptable in his village, no physician heals those who know him.

Jesus said: A city being built on a high mountain and fortified cannot fall nor can it ever be hidden.

Jesus said: What thou shalt hear in thine ear and in the other ear, that preach from your housetops; for no one lights a lamp and puts it under a bushel, nor does he put it in a hidden place, but he sets it on the lampstead, so that all who come in and go out may see its light.

Jesus said: If a blind man leads a blind man, both of them fall into a pit.

Jesus said: It is not possible for one to enter the hosue of the strong man and take him or it by force unless he bind his hands; then will he ransack his house.

Jesus said: Take no thought from morning until evening and from evening until morning for what you shall put on.

His disciples said: When wilt thou be revealed to us and when will we see thee? Jesus said: When you take off your clothing without being ashamed, and take off your clothes and put them under your feet as the little children and tread on them, then shall you behold the Son of the Living One and you shall not fear.

Jesus said: Many times have you desired to hear those words which I say to you, and you have no other from whom to hear them. There will be days when you will seek me and you will not find me.

Jesus said: The Pharisees and the Scribes have received keys of knowledge, they have hidden them. They did not let those enter who wished. But you, become wise as serpents and innocent as doves.

Jesus said: A vine has been planted without the Father and it is not established, it will be pulled up by its roots and be destroyed.

Jesus said: Whoever has in his hand, to him shall be given; and whoever does not have, from him shall be taken even the little which he has.

Jesus said: Whoever blasphemes against the Father, it shall be forgiven him, and whoever blasphemes against the Son, it shall be forgiven him; but whoever blasphemes against the Holy Ghost, it shall not be forgiven him, either on earth or in heaven.

Jesus said: They do not harvest the grapes from thorns, nor do they gather figs from thistles; for they give no fruit. A good man brings forth good out of his treasure, an evil man brings forth evil things out of his evil treasure, which is in his heart, and speaks evil things.

Although there are a number of familiar parables in the Gospel of Thomas, such as the story of the sower, and although Jesus' sayings from the Biblical Gospels also occur, such as the beam in the eye, the lamp under the bushel, and the prophet not being recognised in his own land, much is completely new.

The Gospel is simply a list of Jesus' sayings, devoid of detail, which initially makes it seem less authentic than the more embellished Biblical Gospels. However, since the nineteenth century many eminent scholars have questioned the authenticity of the Evangelists' accounts. Matthew, Mark, Luke and John may have elaborated a similar list of Jesus' sayings based on second- or third-hand reports.

For centuries the four Gospels were unquestioned as contemporary, first-hand accounts. In 1835, however, David Friedrich Strauss published his *Life of Jesus Critically Examined*, which opened up the entire question of Biblical authenticity. Slowly but surely a number of mainstream Biblical scholars began to doubt that the Gospel writers really were eye-witnesses to the events they were describing.

No original manuscript survives from which to accurately date the Gospels. The oldest New Testament to survive is the fourth-century *Codex Sinaiticus* from St Catherine's Monastery at Mount Sinai. A few earlier fragments of the Gospels do survive, but even the oldest of these – the *Rylands Fragment*, containing six verses from St John's Gospel – only dates from around AD 125, almost a century after Christ is thought to have lived. As the oldest complete Bible dates from around the same time as the Nag-Hamadi text, and the *Rylands Fragment* dates from around the same period as the *Oxytrhynchus Fragment* (see p. 113), from a purely historical perspective the Gospel of Thomas has as much claim to authenticity as the Biblical Gospels.

We are left with the content of the Gospels themselves to make their own case. From this standpoint, they do not bear close examination. Matthew, Mark, Luke and John all contain glaring discrepancies. A typical example is the account of Christ's healing of the centurion's servant at Capernaum. In Matthew's Gospel (8:5) it is the centurion himself who approaches Jesus for help:

> And when Jesus was entering Capernaum, there came unto him a centurion, beseeching him.

According to Luke, however, (7:3), the centurion sends a group of Jewish elders to meet with Jesus:

119

And when he heard of Jesus, he sent unto him the elders of the Jews
beseeching him.

There are many other discrepancies between the Gospels which suggest
that the Evangelists had not known Jesus personally. Matthew, for
instance, says that it is Joseph to whom Jesus' coming birth is first
revealed, whereas in Luke's account the Annunciation is made to Mary.
Matthew and Luke also disagree on the name of Joseph's father:
Matthew calls him Jacob and Luke calls him Heli. Most remarkably of
all, however, all four Gospels completely disagree about the most
important event in Christian theology – the Resurrection. They each give
very different versions of the discovery of the empty tomb. According to
Chapter 16 of Mark's Gospel:

And when the Sabbath was past, Mary Magdalene, and Mary the
mother of James and Salome, had brought sweet spices so that they
might come and annoint him . . . And entering into the sepulchre
they saw a young man sitting on the right side, clothed in a long
white garment.

In Luke, Chapter 24, a woman called Joanna and 'other women' are also
present with the two Marys when they enter the sepulchre. This time
there is not one man in the tomb but two:

And it came to pass, as they were much perplexed thereabout,
behold, two men stood by them in shining garments.

In both these accounts, the women arrive to discover the stone already
removed from the entrance to the tomb. In Chapter 28 of Matthew's
Gospel, however, the two Marys actually witness the event:

And behold, there was a great earthquake: for the angel of the Lord
descended from heaven, and came and rolled back the stone from
the door and sat upon it.

Finally, St John has a different version of events entirely. In Chapter 20,
Mary Magdalene arrives alone to find the stone already removed and the
tomb empty. She runs to tell Peter and another unnamed disciple, and
they return with her. After they leave, Mary looks into the sepulchre:

120

And seeth two angles, one at the head, and one at the feet, where the
body of Jesus had lain.

At the very best, only one of these Gospels can be right.

It is now generally agreed by Biblical scholars that the Gospels were
not written until some years after Jesus' time, in the late first or early
second century. Even the earliest estimates place the oldest Gospel,
John's, to around AD 50, some two decades after the events occurred.
What probably happened is that sayings of Jesus were handed down
verbally for a generation or two, until they were committed to writing by
the Evagelists. This does not make them deceitful – they never claimed
to have been present – they merely wrote what they had learned from
others. The Gospel of Thomas, therefore, may have been an original list
of Jesus' sayings, unfettered by the inclusion of half-remembered
events.

The debate concerning the Gospel of Thomas will no doubt continue.
However, the fact still remains that the Gnostics believed that the Gospel
contained Jesus' secret words – a tradition that seems to have influenced
the Grail romances. Here, the Gospel of Thomas almost certainly
became the Holy Grail in *La Folie Perceval* – seemingly the original
romance. In the story Perceval inherits the Holy Grail – the Gospel of
Didymus – and the Gospel of Thomas *is* the Gospel of Didymus.
Regardless of what the Grail later became, or even if the words in
Thomas' Gospel were ever really spoken by Jesus himself, in reading the
above passages we may have seen for ourselves the original Holy Grail.

Summary.

- In 1945, at Nag-Hamadi in Upper Egypt, two Arab farmers uncovered
  a fourth-century copy of the Gospel of Thomas – a Gnostic text
  containing 114 secret sayings of Jesus. The Gospel of Thomas almost
  certainly became the Holy Grail in *La Folie Perceval* – seemingly the
  original romance. In the story Perceval inherits the Holy Grail – the
  Gospel of Didymus – and the Gospel of Thomas *is* the Gospel of
  Didymus.

- The Gospel of Thomas is simply a list of Jesus' sayings, devoid of
  detail, which makes it appear less authentic than the more detailed
  Biblical Gospels. However, many eminent scholars have questioned

the authenticity of the Evangelists' accounts. Matthew, Mark, Luke and John may have elaborated a similar list of Jesus' sayings based on second- or third-hand reports.

- No original manuscript survives from which to accurately date the four Gospels. The oldest New Testament to survive is the fourth-century *Codex Sinaiticus* from St Catherine's Monastery at Mount Sinai. A few earlier fragments of the Gospels do survive, but even the oldest of these – the *Rylands Fragment*, containing six verses from St John's Gospel – only dates from around AD 125, almost a century after Christ is thought to have lived.

- We are left with the content of the Gospels themselves to make their own case. From this standpoint, they do not bear close examination. Matthew, Mark, Luke and John contain glaring discrepancies. A typical example is the account of Christ's healing of the centurion's servant at Capernaum. In Matthew's Gospel it is the centurion himself who approaches Jesus for help, whereas in Luke's Gospel it is a group of Jewish elders.

- There are many other discrepancies between the Gospels which suggest that the Evangelists had not known Jesus personally. Matthew, for example, says that it is Joseph to whom Jesus' coming birth is first revealed, whereas in Luke's account the Annunciation is made to Mary. Matthew and Luke also disagree on the name of Joseph's father: Matthew calls him Jacob and Luke calls him Heli. Most remarkably of all, however, all four Gospels completely disagree about the most important event in Christian theology – the Resurrection. They each give very different versions of the discovery of the empty tomb. At the very best, only one of these Gospels can be right.

- It is now generally agreed that the Gospels were not written until some years after Jesus' time, in the late first or early second century. Even the earliest estimates place the oldest Gospel, John's, to around AD 50, some two decades after the events occurred. What probably happened is that sayings of Jesus were handed down verbally for a generation or two, until they were committed to writing by the Evangelists. The Gospel of Thomas, therefore, may have been an original list of Jesus' sayings, unfettered by the inclusion of half-remembered events.

Chapter XIV

Marian the Chalice

Although the Gospel of Thomas may have been considered *the* Holy Grail when the first of the romances were written, by the late Middle Ages the true Grail was the cup of Christ. We have seen how this appears to have been based around the historical Marian Chalice. As the Gospel of Thomas still exists, then perhaps the Marian Chalice survives too. If my conclusions are correct, the latter was handed down via the descendants of Owain Ddantgwyn until it came into the possession of Payne Peveril's great-grandson Fulk Fitz Warine around the year 1200.

According to *Fulke le Fitz Waryn*, Fulk eventually asked his wife Maude to have the Grail cup relocated in what we are told was its final resting place, a wood about ten miles to the east of Whittington at Alberbury. He then paid for a priory to be built to contain it:

> Fulk founded a priory in the honour of our lady St Mary of the order
> of Grandmont near Alberbury, in a wood, on the river Severn; and it
> is called New Abbey. And not long after he died, and he and Dame
> Maude de Cause, his wife, were interred in this priory.

Just why he chose this site is not explained. However, it is a real historical location. The Priory of St Mary near Alberbury is recorded in the ecclesiastical archives of Canterbury Cathedral. It was eventually taken over by Cistercian monks, but was abandoned after the dissolution of the monasteries. Now called the White Abbey, its ruined walls were incorporated into a farmhouse erected in the mid nineteenth century which still stands beside the B4393, about eight miles west of Shrewsbury.

Did a splendid holy relic, once thought to be the Grail, still remain hidden in the foundations of the old farmhouse? Or had some later member of the Peveril family had it removed. Perhaps an outsider had discovered the artefact, having read *Fulke le Fitz Waryn*. However, *Fulke le Fitz Waryn* was not published until the mid nineteenth century. The surviving copy, now in the British Library, was discovered in the private collection of the Vernon family of Hodnet Hall in north Shropshire in the early 1800s. Interestingly, it was this same family who owned the site of the White Abbey until the farm was built.

It turned out that the Vernon family were directly descended from Fulk and the Peverils. During the reign of Henry VIII, the Fitz Warines sold Whittington Castle and moved to Bath, where their last son, Henry, the fifth Earl of Bath, died without issue. His sister Mary returned to Shropshire and married the squire of Hodnet Hall, Richard Vernon. It was via their son Robert that my investigation into the Grail mystery took on an astonishing new dimension.

Robert Vernon, it seems, became obsessed with the history of his mother's side of the family. He left many papers and diaries describing his research tracing back his lineage through the Fitz Warines to the Peverils. It seems to have been Robert Vernon who discovered the original copy of *Fulke le Fitz Waryn*. In the 1590s Vernon's sister Elizabeth married Shakespeare's patron, the Earl of Southampton, and Vernon himself became involved with the theatre. He even tried his hand as a poet and playwright, and for a time worked at the Shoreditch Theatre where Shakespeare himself was working. There is no evidence that he ever collaborated with Shakespeare, but he did patronise Shakespeare's fellow playwright Anthony Munday.

Robert Vernon was inspired to write his own romantic portrayal of Fulk Fitz Warine's life. Called *The Quest of Fulk Fitz Warine*, it is still preserved in the William Salt Collection in Stafford. Vernon must have based his story on *Fulke le Fitz Waryn*, as parts of the romance are included almost word for word. Like *Fulke le Fitz Waryn*, Vernon's quest concerns Fulk's adventures. However, he portrays Fulk in a remarkable way. He not only casts him as an Arthurian heir – but also as Robin Hood.

For some reason Vernon wrote the story in French, but in English translation his introduction reads:

This Fulk was in truth the notorious outlaw Robin Hood. He was cast from his lands by the villainous King John, and was forced to join with rebellious cut-throats in the forest of Babbinswood. He took the name of Robin Hood as he would keep the truth of his identity a secret, lest the King did pursue him unto death . . . He was descended from Arthur, the great king of the Britons, but is reduced now to the life of an outlaw. Only should his quest succeed will he regain his inheritance, for he must find his Marian.

Robin Hood a descendant of King Arthur! This was a new one to me. I was familiar with a number of early Robin Hood stories, dating from the fifteenth century, but nowhere had I found him linked with Arthur. Vernon was not alone, however, in linking Robin Hood with Fulk Fizt Warine. The eighteenth-century Shropshire antiquarian Simon Pearson had also described Fulk as the 'Shropshire Robin Hood'. Additionally, in the late nineteenth century another Shropshire historian, William Cathrall, in his *History of Oswestry*, believed that the Robin Hood children's tale 'Babes in the Wood' originated with the name 'Babbinswood', the forest around Whittington where Fulk Fitz Warine had been an outlaw.

As I continued to search through the available literature linking Robin Hood with Fulk Fitz Warine, I discovered something incredible. In the William Salt Collection there exists a Robin Hood poem thought to have been composed by an anonymous Shropshire ballad writer around 1550. Entitled *Robin and Marian*, all that now survives are a few verses scribbled on the back of a letter. Although Fulk is not mentioned by name, the theme is similar to Vernon's in that Robin goes in search of 'his beloved Marian'. Astonishingly, in this story Marian is not a person but 'a chalice, the most costly ever made'.

I had concluded that the historical Grail was the Marian Chalice; *Fulke le Fitz Waryn* had linked Fulk with the Grail; Vernon had linked Fulk with Robin Hood; and now another sixteenth-century writer had linked Robin Hood with a chalice named Marian. This must be more than coincidence.

Unfortunately, only a few verses of the Robin and Marian poem survive, so there is no way of knowing what this chalice was meant to be. Nevertheless, where had the author got the idea to make Marian into a chalice? It was then that I realised that nowhere in *The Quest of Fulk Fitz Warine* does Vernon introduce Marian personally into his narrative. Vernon left the story unfinished; at least the surviving copy is incomplete. In what does survive we are simply told that Fulk 'must find his Marian', and the story continues with his adventures during this quest. Could Vernon's Marian also be a chalice?

Surprisingly, although the earliest surviving Robin Hood stories date from around 1400, Marian fails to feature in any of them for about two hundred years. The first writer to include her as Robin's lover was the playwright Anthony Munday – the very writer patronised by Robert Vernon.

I was definitely on to something: in the 1550s a Shropshire writer portrays Marian as a chalice; around 1600 Robert Vernon, another Shropshire writer, includes her in his story without saying what she is; and almost at the same time Vernon's associate Munday first introduces Maid Marian into the Robin Hood story. Had Munday copied the name from Vernon, wrongly assuming Marian to be a woman? It certainly seems that something influenced Munday to introduce the name Marian as an afterthought, as his heroine's true name is given as Matilda. Only when she flees to the greenwood to join Robin as an outlaw does she adopt the name Marian in order to protect her true identity.

By the early weeks of 1994 my line of investigation had moved into totally unchartered waters. If Marian in the Robin Hood story was originally the Marian Chalice and not a woman, then the solution to the Grail mystery might be found not with the legend of King Arthur, but with the legend of Robin Hood. Was Fulk Fitz Warine really the historical Robin Hood as Vernon believed? Firstly, I needed to discover how the traditional Robin Hood legend originated.

In England in 1193, with Richard the Lionheart fighting in Palestine, the King's trusted friend Robin Hood, the Earl of Huntingdon, was cast from his lands by the treacherous Prince John. Outlawed and pursued into Sherwood Forest by the ruthless Sheriff of Nottingham, Robin raised a valiant band of followers, stole from the Norman rich to give to the poor, and became the hero of the Saxon peasants.

This, the story of Robin Hood as we know it today, originated with the Elizabethan playwright Anthony Munday in 1598. Contemporary with the works of Shakespeare, Munday's two plays, *The Downfall of Robert, Earl of Huntingdon* and *The Death of Robert the Earl of Huntingdon*, were as popular as any of Shakespeare's works, which ensured that this incarnation of the Robin Hood story survived. However, although Munday portrayed Robin as the Earl of Huntingdon, he did not invent the

Robin Hood story. The oldest known reference to Robin Hood is contained in a work composed two and a half centuries earlier, in 1377, by the London cleric-poet William Langland. In his poems *Piers the Ploughman* Langland notes in passing, 'I know the rhymes of Robin Hood'. Unfortunately, Langland tells us no more about the outlaw, and the rhymes to which he refers have not survived.

The oldest extant Robin Hood story survives in the form of a ballad now preserved in the Advocates Library in Edinburgh. Called *A Gest of Robyn Hode* (or the *Gest* for short), it first appeared in print around 1510, but from linguistic analysis scholars have concluded that it might originally have been composed around the year 1400.

The *Gest* opens in the outlaw's camp, where Robin refuses to dine until he is accompanied by a guest of honour, a rich traveller whom they can rob to pay for the banquet. On Robin's orders Little John, Much and Will Scarlet waylay a downcast knight, who is brought to the camp. The knight says that he has little money, having been forced to sell his possessions to repay the abbot of St Mary's Abbey in York. He has mortgaged his estates to the abbot to secure the release of his son, unjustly imprisoned for murder. Sympathetic to the knight's cause, Robin lends him £400 and sends him on his way.

Eventually, the Sheriff of Nottingham decides to capture the outlaws by staging an archery contest to attract the finest archers of the north, the prize for the winner being a magnificent arrow of gold and silver. The band enter the contest in disguise, but when Robin is victorious the sheriff orders their arrest. Although Little John is wounded by an arrow in the leg, the outlaws escape and flee to the castle of the knight, who repays them by offering them protection.

When the sheriff arrives, the knight refuses to release Robin unless ordered to do so by the King himself. Petitioned by the sheriff, the King agrees to come to Nottingham to personally ensure the capture of Robin Hood and the renegade knight. However, while the sheriff is away, Robin and the outlaws escape and return to the forest. Ultimately, the knight is arrested, although he is later rescued by Robin, who kills the sheriff.

The King arrives in Nottingham and, discovering the sheriff dead, attempts to seize the knight's lands. Disguised as an abbot, with his men as monks, the King enters the forest to hunt down Robin himself. When the outlaws intercept the party, Robin unwittingly demonstrates his allegiance to the King, and the King reveals his true identity. Impressed by the show of loyalty, the King offers amnesty to Robin and his men, who return with him to Nottingham, while the knight returns to his castle.

Finally, Robin enters the King's service at court, where he remains for fifteen months until, homesick, he returns to the forest. For twenty-two years he lives as an outlaw in the greenwood; ultimately, he is beguiled by the treacherous prioress of Kirklees who betrays him to his enemy Sir Roger of Doncaster.

What can be deduced regarding the original Robin Hood legend from this early ballad? Composed over a century – perhaps two – before Anthony Munday's plays gave us the modern version of the story, the ballad reveals a very different Robin Hood from the character we know today. He is portrayed not as a disinherited earl, but as a peasant who has taken up arms against the authorities.

The Kirklees prioress is the only woman to appear in the early ballads. As for Maid Marian, she had absolutely nothing to do with this original Robin Hood story. She is not recorded in any of the surviving stories of Robin Hood before Munday's plays in the late sixteenth century. Even then, as mentioned earlier, her true name is Matilda. The full title of the first of Munday's Robin Hood plays was: *The Downfall of Robert, Earl of Huntingdon, afterwards called Robin Hood of merry Sherwood: with his love to chaste Matilda, the Lord Fitzwater's daughter, afterwards his fair Maid Marian.* In the play Matilda assumes the disguise of a peasant woman named Marian once she has fled to the forest to join her lover.

The oldest reference anywhere to Marian in association with Robin Hood is in the poem fragment, *Robin and Marian*, in the William Salt Collection. As we have seen, it dates from around 1550, fifty years before Munday's play appeared. In this poem Marian is not a woman but a chalice. The next oldest reference to Marian in association with Robin Hood are found in Robert Vernon's *Quest of Fulk Fitz Warine* and Munday's play, both of which were written around 1600. As we have seen, Munday may have got the name Marian from his patron, Vernon himself. In the latter's story we are not told anything about Marian, merely that Robin must find her in order to regain his inheritance. The Robin Hood in Vernon's story is not the Sherwood outlaw, however, but Fulk Fitz Warine. In *Fulke le Fitz Waryn* Fulk must find the Grail in order to regain *his* inheritance. Marian and the Grail seem, therefore, to be one and the same.

As the anonymous *Robin and Marian* of 1550 was also set in Fulk's home county of Shropshire, it seems that Marian originally had absolutely nothing to do with the Sherwood Robin Hood legend, but was associated solely with the story of Fulk Fitz Warine, where the name applies to a chalice. As far as is known, the only chalice ever recorded with the name Marian was the Marian Chalice taken from Rome in AD 410 – the chalice that seems to have been the original Holy Grail cup. Historically, it seems that Fulk's ancestors did possess the Marian Chalice, and in the medieval romance *Fulke le Fitz Waryn* Fulk discovers the Holy Grail. Fulk's Marian, the original Marian, therefore appears to have been the Holy Grail. Vernon's friend Munday, however, used the name for the assumed identity of Robin's lover Matilda; the name stuck, and to this day Maid Marian is still the heroine of the Robin Hood story. But what of Fulk Fitz Warine? Why did Vernon say he was Robin Hood?

Summary

- Although the Gospel of Thomas may have been considered *the* Holy Grail when the first of the romances were written, by the late Middle Ages the true Grail was the cup of Christ. This legend appears to have been based around the historical Marian Chalice, handed down via the descendants of Owain Ddantgwyn until it came into the possession of Payne Peveril's great-grandson Fulk Fitz Warine around the year 1200.

- Around 1600, Fulk's direct descendant Robert Vernon, of Hodnet in Shropshire, was inspired to write his own romantic portrayal of Fulk's life. Called *The Quest of Fulk Fitz Warine*, it portrays him in a remarkable way. Vernon not only says that Fulk was a descendant of King Arthur, he also says that he was the historical Robin Hood. Vernon seems to have taken his story from an anonymous Shropshire ballad called *Robin and Marian* (*circa* 1550), in which Robin is portrayed as a disinherited Shropshire baron. However, in this story Marian is not a person but 'a chalice, the most costly ever made'.

- Although the earliest surviving Robin Hood stories date from around 1400, Marian fails to feature in any of them for about two hundred years. The first writer to include her as Robin's lover was the Elizabethan playwright Anthony Munday – a writer who was

129

patronised by Robert Vernon. Perhaps Munday copied the name from Vernon, wrongly assuming Marian to be a woman?

- In Vernon's story we are not told anything about Marian, merely that Robin must find her in order to regain his inheritance. The Robin Hood in Vernon's story is not the Sherwood outlaw, however, but Fulk Fitz Warine. In *Fulke le Fitz Waryn* Fulk must find the Grail in order to regain *his* inheritance. Marian and the Grail seem, therefore, to be one and the same. As far as it known, the only chalice ever recorded with the name Marian was the Marian Chalice taken from Rome in AD 410 – the chalice that seems to have been the original Grail cup.

Chapter XV

The Legend of Robin Hood

Anthony Munday could well have based his disinherited earl, the sworn enemy of King John, on Fulk Fitz Warine. In Munday's play Matilda, lecherously pursued by King John, follows Robin to Sherwood and becomes an outlaw. Historically, King John had designs on Maude de Caus, Fulk's wife. She too joined Fulk in the forest as an outlaw. Also, like Robin, Fulk is eventually reinstated and helps force the King to sign the Magna Carta. Munday, however, sets his story in Nottinghamshire, and includes the familiar characters from the original ballads. Consequently, it is a hybrid story, mixing the legendary outlaws Robin of Sherwood and Fulk of Shropshire.

Munday probably got the idea of basing his hero on Fulk Fitz Warine from Robert Vernon. But why should Vernon think that Fulk was Robin Hood in the first place? Is there any historical evidence that he was associated with the Robin Hood legend before Vernon's work? The early ballads are set in Sherwood in Nottinghamshire, and the original hero was a yeoman rather an aristocrat. Was there, however, a parallel legend portraying Robin as a disinherited earl? If so, was it connected with Fulk Fitz Warine?

The oldest surviving reference to a Robin Hood having lived in the twelfth century was made by the Scottish writer John Major in 1521. Major was convinced that Robin Hood was an historical figure, stating in his *History of Greater Britain* that Robin was outlawed between 1193 and 1194 while Richard I was held captive in Germany after his crusade to the Holy Land. Major continued Robin's life through the reign of King John (1199–1216) and into the reign of Henry III (1216–1272), dating his death to 18 November 1247, aged eighty-seven.

Around 1560, some forty years after Major's reference, the printer Richard Grafton also announced that he had found evidence that Robin

Hood was an historical outlaw during the reign of Richard I and King John. However, although Grafton claimed to have discovered an 'old and authentic pamphlet' dating Robin's life to around 1200, as well as records in the Exchequer rolls concerning the confiscation of the outlaw's lands, he failed to produce either as proof, or more importantly say where Robin originated. By the end of the sixteenth century, Major's and Grafton's dating had become generally accepted. Anthony Munday then set his plays during that period, thus establishing the historical setting for all the subsequent Robin Hood tales. In 1795 the antiquarian Joseph Ritson gave the nineteenth-century romantic novelists their final authority for dating, also giving the year 1160 for Robin's birth.

As the early ballads clearly concern a Robin Hood who had no aristocratic connections, who did these later writers consider to have been the original hero? The answer may lie with William Langland's *Piers the Ploughman*. In it he wrote: 'I know the rhymes of Robin Hood and Randolf Earl of Chester.' The Randolf referred to was the third Earl of Chester (1172–1232), who lived during the reigns of Richard I and King John. Since Robin and Randolf are coupled in the same passage, it appears they were thought to have lived at the same time and fought side by side. Who was the Robin Hood referenced in Langland's poem?

It may well have been Fulk Fitz Warine: he was the only historical outlaw leader alongside whom Randolf fought. When Fulk was dispossessed by King John in favour of John's friend Moris Fitz Roger, he raised an army from among the local people of Shropshire and reoccupied Whittington Castle. King John then sent Randolf, the Earl of Chester, with an army to seize Whittington. However, Randolf changed sides, joined with Fulk and fought along side him in his guerrilla campaign against King John. The full story is included in *Fulke le Fitz Waryn*; however, the story also includes far more to link Fulk with the legendary Robin Hood.

Born in the 1170s, Fulk became lord of Whittington on the death of his father in 1197. However, Moris Fitz Roger successfully claimed Whittington Castle and Fulk was outlawed by King John on a trumped-up charge of treason in 1200. For the next three years he fought against the King in the forests of Shropshire and in the marshes of north-central Wales. Pardoned in 1203, Fulk inherited Whittington, although in 1215 he again rebelled in support of the baronial revolt which led to the signing of the Magna Carta. He quickly became a popular folk hero,

132

having successfully rebelled against the unpopular King John on two occasions.

The romance *Fulke le Fitz Waryn*, composed around 1260, focuses mainly on Fulk's life in the three years between 1200 and 1203, when he was engaged in his first campaign against the King. After an initial section outlining Fulk's right to Whittington Castle, the hero himself enters the story. He is playing a game of chess with the future King John when a quarrel erupts. Fulk assaults John and the prince swears revenge. John is powerless to act immediately, as King Richard is a friend of the Fitz Warine family. When Richard dies, however, and John becomes king, he exacts vengeance by giving Whittington to Fulk's enemy Sir Moris Fitz Roger.

Disinherited and outlawed, Fulk and his followers flee from Whittington to nearby Babbinswood Forest. In the forest, Fulk gathers about him others who have grievances against the King and Sir Moris, and together they attack Whittington Castle. The siege fails and the outlaws flee, Fulk being wounded in the leg by an arrow. When his wound has healed, he continues to make trouble for Moris and the King by robbing wealthy merchants in the forests of Shropshire. He soon becomes a popular hero throughout the district, promising to steal only from the King's friends.

Fulk's brother John eventually tricks Sir Moris and lures him into the forest, where he is attacked and killed by the outlaws. The King's anger turns to fury when Fulk rescues and marries Maude de Caus, the richest and fairest lady in England, with whom the King is infatuated. With his new bride Fulk returns to the forest. Deciding to defeat Fulk himself, the King marches north from Winchester, but the outlaws are granted asylum at Castle Balham near Shrewsbury by a friendly knight called Sir Lewis. In the ensuing battle the King is forced to retreat and Fulk returns to his castle at Whittington.

Fulk's good fortune does not last, however, for the King appoints the ruthless knight Henry de Audley of Red Castle (at Hawkstone Park, near Hodnet) as sheriff. With ten thousand knights, Sir Henry besieges Whittington, and Fulk and his men barely escape alive. After a series of adventures the outlaws flee to the Continent, where they enter the service of the French king.

When they return to England, Fulk travels to Windsor where King John is holding court. Disguised as a peasant, he offers to lead the King to a good hunting spot in the forest. When the King accepts the invitation and enters the forest, he is captured by the outlaws and made to promise that he will no longer pursue them. Although he agrees, the moment he is free the oath is broken.

King John's final attempt to capture Fulk involves enlisting the help of Randolf, the Earl of Chester. Randolf is considered the greatest warrior in the land, but even this plan backfires on the King. Randolf joins forces with Fulk and they share many adventures together. Ultimately, Fulk captures the King in the New Forest, making him swear to reinstate him. On this occasion King John keeps his word, and Fulk and his family return to Whittington. It is at this point in the story that Fulk goes in search of the Grail.

It is clear that Munday acquired many of his themes for the later Robin Hood tale from the story of Fulk Fitz Warine; for example, the disinherited lord and his faithful lover, pursued by the lecherous Prince John until she herself becomes an outlaw. However, the tale of *Fulke le Fitz Waryn* has even more in common with the very earliest of the Robin Hood stories, the *Gest*.

Significantly, the stories of *Fulke le Fitz Waryn* and the *Gest* are in parts almost identical. Both Fulk and Robin's right-hand men are called John; Little John is Robin's lieutenant, while Fulk's is his brother John. In both stories John is instructed to waylay a party of wealthy travellers and bring them back to the camp to dine. In the *Gest* it is a party of monks from St Mary's Abbey:

> The monks had fifty two men,
> And seven laden horse full strong,
> There rides no bishop in this land,
> So royally, I understand.

In the tale of *Fulke le Fitz Waryn*, the victims are a group of merchants carrying the King's wealth:

> Then came from abroad ten burger merchants, who had bought with the money of the king of England the richest cloths, furs, spices and gloves . . . and they were carrying them under the forest towards the king.

In the *Gest* Robin instructs John to intercept the party:

> And walk up into Sayles,

And so to Watling Street,
And wait for some unknown guest,
By chance you may then meet.

In *Fulke le Fitz Waryn* the scene is thematically similar.

> When Fulk perceived the merchants, he called his brother John, and
> told him to go and talk with these people and inquire of what land
> they were.

In both tales, the respective Johns intercept the party and take them back
to their leader's camp. The prisoners dine with the outlaws, thereafter
being made to pay with their belongings. Both Fulk and Robin set their
prisoners free, instructing them to thank their masters for the proceeds of
the robbery. In the *Gest*:

> Greet well your abbot, said Robin,
> And your prior, I you pray,
> And bid him send me such a monk,
> To dinner every day.

In *Fulke le Fitz Waryn*:

> He bade them adieu, and prayed them to salute the king from Fulk
> Fitz Warine, who thanked him much for his good robes.

In the initial section of the Fulk story the villain is Sir Moris, whose
encounter with the outlaws bears a marked resemblance to that of the
sheriff with Robin's men. In the *Gest* John goes to Nottingham in
disguise to outwit the sheriff by becoming one of his men; in *Fulke le
Fitz Waryn* John goes to the White Town in disguise, to trick Sir Moris in
exactly the same way. Even the manner of the Johns' meetings with the
respective villains are almost identical. In the *Gest* the sheriff questions
John about his origins:

> In what country were you born,
> And where is your dwelling place.
> In Holderness, sir, I was born.

In *Fulke le Fitz Waryn*, Sir Moris questions John in precisely the same way:

> Moris asked him where he was born. 'Sir,' said he, 'in the march of Scotland.'

Subsequently, both Johns gain the confidence of their enemies, luring them into the forest and into a trap. In the *Gest* the sheriff is humiliated, but allowed to go free, but in *Fulke le Fitz Waryn* Moris is killed.

Earlier in the Fulk story, the outlaws are fleeing from Moris' men, in a similar manner to the flight of Robin's outlaws after the archery contest in the *Gest*. When Robin's outlaws are fleeing from the sheriff, Little John is wounded:

> Little John was hurt full sore,
> With an arrow in his knee.

In *Fulke le Fitz Waryn* it is Fulk himself who is wounded in the leg while fleeing from sir Moris:

> At length came Morgan Fitz Aaron, and shot from the castle, and struck Fulk through the leg with an arrow.

In *Fulke le Fitz Waryn*, Sir Moris eventually goes to the King for help:

> Sir Moris made his complaint to the king ... the king became so incensed that ... he appointed a hundred knights with their company to go through all England, to seek and take Fulk.

In the *Gest*, the Sheriff of Nottingham also appeals to the King:

> Forth he rode to London town,
> All for to tell the king ...
> I will be at Nottingham, said the king ...
> And take I will Robin Hood.

Like the Sheriff, Moris is eventually killed by the hero. With Moris dead, King John comes personally to challenge Fulk, as does King Edward when the sheriff dies in the *Gest*. In the *Gest*, the outlaws find temporary

136

sanctuary with the friendly knight, Sir Richard at the Lee, as do Fulk's men at the castle of Sir Lewis in Shrewsbury. Furthermore, when King John arrives in Shropshire, he finds it impossible to raise support because of the fear and respect the local people have for Fulk, just as King Edward discovers he can find no one willing to help him seize the castle of the knight who is protected by Robin Hood.

In *Fulke le Fitz Waryn*, with Moris dead, King John assumes the role of arch enemy. Once again, his encounters with the outlaws echo those of the sheriff in the *Gest*. In the *Gest* a disguised Little John meets the sheriff in the forest, telling him he knows where good hunting is to be found:

> I have been in this forest,
> A fair sight can I see,
> It was one of the fairest sights
> That I have ever seen.
>
> Yonder I see a right fair hart,
> . . . follow and come with me.

The same ploy is used by Fulk when he too encounters his enemy in disguise:

> 'Sir villain,' said the king, 'have you seen no stag or doe pass here?' 'Yes, my lord, a while ago.' 'What beast did you see?' 'Sir, my lord, a horned one; and it had long horns.' 'Where is it?' 'Sir, my lord, I know very well how to lead you to where I saw it.'

Both arch enemies are then led into a trap, captured and humiliated. Eventually, both the sheriff and King John promise to harm the outlaws no longer, in both instances immediately breaking the oath the moment they are free.

Towards the end of both stories, Robin and Fulk are reunited with their respective kings. Fulk's lands are returned and Robin enters the King's service. Ultimately, Robin wishes to return to the forest and visit a chapel he founded in Barnsdale. He appeals to the King to grant him leave:

> I made a chapel in Barnsdale,
> That seemly is to see,

> It is of Mary Magdalene,
> And thereto would I be.

Similarly, Fulk founds a priory dedicated to St Mary:

> [Fulk] founded a priory in the honour of our lady St Mary of the order of Grandmont near Alberbury, in a wood, on the River Severn; and it is called the New Abbey.

Other early Robin Hood ballads are also echoed in *Fulke le Fitz Waryn*. Fulk leaves his men and goes to Canterbury Cathedral to pray alone, a remarkably similar theme to Robin's lone visit to St Mary's Church in Nottingham in *Robin Hood and the Monk*, another ballad written in the early fifteenth century.

The similarities occur too frequently, and too nearly identically, to be coincidental. Clearly one story has been taken from the other, but which came first? In its present form, the *Gest* was not committed to writing until the fifteenth century, whereas *Fulke le Fitz Waryn* was written around 1260. The surviving copy of *Fulke le Fitz Waryn* is thus certainly older. The writer of the *Gest* must, therefore, have drawn upon events from the life of Fulk Fitz Warine to elaborate his own story of Robin Hood, whether or not there was an historical outlaw who ever bore that name. By the sixteenth century Fulk's connection with the Robin Hood story seems to have been all but forgotten; Robert Vernon, however, evidently knew all about it.

As Vernon had been so accurate concerning Fulk and his link with the Robin Hood legend, perhaps he could shed more light on the Grail mystery. Remember, Vernon was Fulk's direct descendant, and therefore, if my theory was right, the successor to the Grail guardians. The more I discovered about Robert Vernon, the more I became convinced that he too believed that the Grail cup referenced in *Fulke le Fitz Waryn* was a genuine historical relic. Moreover, it seems that Vernon had attempted to find it for himself.

Summary

- It is clear that Anthony Munday (the author of the modern Robin Hood story composed around 1600) acquired many of his themes for his Robin Hood tale from the story of Fulk Fitz Warine. For example, in both stories the disinherited lord's faithful lover is pursued by the lecherous Prince John until she herself becomes an outlaw. However, the tale of *Fulke le Fitz Waryn* has even more in common with the very earliest of the Robin Hood stories, the *Gest*, which was written around 1400.

- Significantly, the stories of *Fulke le Fitz Waryn* and the *Gest* are almost identical in parts. Both Fulk and Robin's right-hand men are called John; Little John is Robin's lieutenant, while Fulk's is his brother John. In both stories John is instructed to waylay a party of wealthy travellers and bring them back to the camp. The prisoners dine with the outlaws, thereafter being made to pay with their belongings. Both Fulk and Robin set their prisoners free, instructing them to thank their masters for the proceeds of the robbery.

- In *Fulke le Fitz Waryn*, the villain is Sir Moris, whose encounter with the outlaws bears a marked resemblance to that of the sheriff with Robin's men. In the *Gest* John goes to Nottingham in disguise to outwit the sheriff by becoming one of his men; in *Fulke le Fitz Waryn* John goes to the White Town in disguise, to trick Sir Moris in exactly the same way.

- Such similarities occur too frequently, and too nearly identically, to be coincidental. Clearly one story has been taken from the other. In its present form, the *Gest* was not committed to writing until the fifteenth century, whereas *Fulke le Fitz Waryn* was written around 1260. The surviving copy of *Fulke le Fitz Waryn* is therefore certainly older. The writer of the *Gest* must have drawn upon events from the life of Fulk Fitz Warine to elaborate his own story of Robin Hood, whether or not there was an historical outlaw who ever bore that name.

- Historical evidence that Fulk was thought to have been Robin Hood in the Middle Ages comes from William Langland's *Piers the Ploughman* of 1377 – the oldest surviving reference to the outlaw. In the poem Langland wrote: 'I know the rhymes of Robin Hood and Randolf Earl of Chester.' The Randolf referred to was the third Earl of Chester (1172–1232) who lived during the reigns of Richard I and King John. Since Robin and Randolf are coupled in the same passage, it appears they were thought to have lived at the same time and fought side by side. The Robin Hood in the poem may well have been Fulk Fitz Warine: he was the only historical outlaw leader alongside whom Randolf fought.

Chapter XVI

The Shepherd's Songs

The Shropshire County Records, in Shrewsbury Central Library, reveal that in 1596 Robert Vernon purchased the site of the White Abbey, where Fulk had hidden the Grail in *Fulke le Fitz Waryn*. The romance had probably been in the private collection of Vernon's mother's family since it was written around 1260. Vernon seems to have been the first member of the family for centuries to have taken any real interest in the story of Fulk and, since Fulk himself was apparently buried in the abbey, his purchase of the property may simply have been due to a desire to own the tomb of his ancestor. However, Vernon's interest did not end there. The abbey was just a ruin by the late sixteenth century, and he began to renovate the entire area. Parts of the crumbling structure were re-erected but, more importantly, large sections of the interior were excavated to landscape the ruins as a scenic garden. I began to wonder if there was more to it. After all, Vernon knew the Fulk Grail legend. Had he hoped to find the Grail in the abbey ruins?

Unfortunately, Vernon left no specific record of the renovation itself. However, he did write about the Grail, connecting it with the White Abbey. Around 1615, shortly before his death, he composed a poem based on the medieval Arthurian romance *Sir Gawain and the Green Knight*. In Vernon's poem, *Sir Gawain and the Red Knight*, he sets the story in the countryside around his home in north Shropshire, and even sites the Grail chapel at the White Abbey. In the story the monks of the White Abbey are the guardians of the Grail, but the Red Knight steals it and takes it to his fortress, the Red Castle. Once again, the Red Castle is an historical building; its red-brick ruins can still be seen at Hawkstone Park, about three miles south-west of Hodnet. Arthur's knight Gawain then offers to help the monks, eventually defeating the Red Knight and retrieving the Grail. However, instead of returning the Grail to the monks, Gawain decides to hide it in some unspecified location. (The original hand-written copy of Vernon's poem no longer survives, but it was published by the Shropshire antiquarian Thomas Wright in 1855.)

Mysteriously, Vernon claimed to have made a remarkable discovery which inspired him to write *Sir Gawain and the Red Knight*. In his introduction to the poem he wrote:

> As the Lord would deem it, I have made at the White Abbey of St Augustine, the finding which has led me to make such verse, for those who have eyes to see, and so worthy seen as I have seen.

Although the precise meaning of the passage is obscure, it seems that Vernon was claiming to have found the Grail. The poem was about the Grail, the White Abbey is where the Grail is kept in the poem, and Vernon says he has found something in the White Abbey which led him to write the poem. What else could 'the finding' be?

Anyone else reading this passage and concluding that Vernon was claiming to have found the Grail is unlikely to have taken him seriously. Even if they believed the Grail to have been a genuine historical relic, they are unlikely to have associated it with the White Abbey. But my research had, independently of Vernon's work, led me to the theory that the Grail was an historical artefact – the Marian Chalice – and that it could well have passed into the hand of Fulk Fitz Warine, who in the romance did hide it in the White Abbey. So had Vernon really found the Grail?

The Vernon baronial line ended in the last century, and the present owners of the Vernon manor at Hodnet Hall, the Heber-Percys, inherited nothing of the Vernons' literary estate. The last person known to have possessed the Vernon family papers was the Shropshire antiquarian Thomas Wright in the mid nineteenth century. Nothing is known of what happened to them after he died in the 1860s. However, Wright did make sure that *Fulke le Fitz Waryn* and both Vernon's *Quest of Fulk Fitz Warine* and his *Sir Gawain and the Red Knight* were published in 1855 by the Warton Club in London.

When I examined the Warton Club edition of *Sir Gawain and the Red Knight* I became intrigued by something that I had first taken to be some kind of printer's reference. The poem ends with Gawain recovering the Grail for the monks, but instead of returning it to the White Abbey, he decides to hide it in a safer location. Strangely, the poem does not say where it was hidden, merely that Gawain stood on the battlements of the Red Castle contemplating its hiding place. The final lines of the poem read:

> The shepherd's songs to guide the way,
> The horn was blown, the treasure lay.

Following these final words there are two lines of letters:

CXXXII XXXI LXI CII CIV CXXXV CXLII CXXIII CXVIII CXIX CXVI
XVII III II XIX VIII II XIX IV I XXII CXIV XIII

They appear to be Roman numerals:

132 31 61 102 104 135 118 142 123 118 119 116
17 3 2 19 8 2 19 4 1 22 114 13

Nowhere in the text or the preface does Vernon make reference to these mysterious numerals. There is no way of knowing if they were at the end of Vernon's original copy. But whoever inserted them, what did they mean? I asked a number of antique book dealers if they could explain, but they were as mystified as I. As the numerals did not seem connected with the printing of the book, I had to assume that they had formed part of the original poem. But why had Vernon included them? I was suddenly reminded of the words from Vernon's introduction to the poem:

. . . . for those who have eyes to see, and so worthy seen as I have seen.

An intriguing idea suddenly struck me: what if Vernon had hidden the Grail before his death and, seeing himself as some latter-day Merlin, left a coded message to reveal its location? In his poem, the Grail had originally been in the White Abbey, but Gawain had hidden it somewhere else. Perhaps Vernon, having found the Grail at the White Abbey, had himself concealed it in some other location. Did the poem secretly contain clues to where this might be? After all, Vernon finished the poem without saying where Gawain had hidden the Grail – all he left were the two lines of numerals. Were these coded instructions? Although I was excited by the possibility, I still expected that the numerals would eventually turn out to be some kind of printer's reference. As an experiment, however, I decided to regard the numbers as a code and began to try to decipher it.

The problem was deciding what the individual numbers might relate to. As the penultimate line of the poem referred to 'the shepherd's songs' guiding the way, 'the shepherd's songs' might be the key to the code. I spent many hours examining poems, rhymes, ballads and hymns which existed in the early seventeenth century when Vernon had written the poem. Eventually, I arrived at a plausible solution to the enigma. If Vernon intended his code to survive, he would surely have chosen references that would remain unaltered for decades, if not for centuries. Rhymes, poems, ballads and hymns are often changed or updated, even forgotten over time. However, one series of songs unlikely to be altered was that included in the Bible – the Psalms. Not only are the Psalms songs, they are *shepherd's songs*, attributed to Hebrew King David, a humble shepherd before he became the Israelite hero after slaying the giant Goliath.

There were two separate lines of numerals in Vernon's poem. Did the first line refer to the number of the Psalm and the second line to the verse? The first number in Vernon's first sequence is 132, and the first number in the second sequence is 17. Psalm 132, verse 17 reads:

There will I make the horn of David to bud: I have ordained a lamp for mine anointed

It seemed beyond coincidence that the verse should refer to the shepherd David and a horn – the poem actually ended with the line, 'the horn was blown'. Was Vernon assuring his reader that he or she was on the right track? The reference to the lamp in the verse may even have been used to indicate a guiding light, the following verses perhaps? Vernon would certainly have been able to use the same Bible translation that I was using, the King James edition printed in 1611, four years before he wrote his poem.

The second numbers in the sequences are 31 and 3: Psalm 31, verse 3 reads:

For thou art my rock and my fortress: therefore for my name's sake lead me, and guide me.

Again the reference seemed to correlate with a search – 'lead me, and guide me' – but where? The verse included a rock and a fortress, and in Vernon's poem Gawain stood on the battlements of the Red Castle. Significantly, the Red Castle, whose ruins still survive, some three miles from Hodnet at Hawkstone Park, is a fortress cut into the rocks. Is this what the conundrum was referring to?

In February 1994 I visited the Red Castle ruins to see if the remaining verses made geographical sense. If my reasoning was correct, then the third reference was Psalm 61, verse 2. The final line of the verse reads:

Lead me to the rock that is higher than I.

From the Red Castle there is only one higher location in the immediate vicinity, the White Cliff, which overlooks the castle about a quarter of a mile to the west. Above the White Cliff, facing the Red Castle, is a ruined chapel. The present ruin is a folly, but a much earlier chapel stood on the site, which is known from a drawing made by the Shropshire antiquarian John Street in 1620. This was within a decade of Vernon writing his poem, so again the location was historically sound.

From the chapel the next reference was consulted. Psalm 102, verse 19 begins:

For he hath looked down from the height of his sanctuary.

Until this point I had considered the associations coincidental. However, I was no longer so sure. 'The height of his sanctuary.' What better way to describe a chapel on the top of a cliff? I looked about me and found a narrow gorge cutting its way towards through the rocks. Did the next reference, Psalm 104, verse 8, refer to this gorge?

They go up by the mountains; they go down by the valleys unto the place which thou hast founded for them.

I followed the gorge to the valley at the bottom, continuing downward until I reached the nearby village of Weston, about a mile away. The next reference was Psalm 135, verse 2, which begins:

Ye that stand in the house of the Lord.

The house of the Lord surely referred to a church, so I made my way to the village parish church. It was medieval, so would certainly have been there in Vernon's day. Remarkably, the next four verses seemed to be telling me exactly what to do. Psalm 118, verse 19:

> Open to me the gates of righteousness: I will go into them.

I entered the church. Psalm 142, verse 4:

> I looked on my right hand and beheld.

I turned to my right. Psalm 123, verse 1:

> Unto thee lift I up mine eyes.

I looked up into the church rafters. Psalm 118, verse 22:

> The stone which the builders refused is become the headstone of the corner.

Had something really been hidden behind the highest stone in the northwest (back right) corner of the church? The penultimate verse seemed to confirm so. Psalm 119, verse 114:

> Thou art my hiding place and my shield: I hope in thy word.

Everything seemed to fit. Unfortunately, if anything had been hidden in that particular church it was long gone. Although a church had stood on the site since the early Middle Ages, and could therefore have been included in Robert Vernon's conundrum, the present building dated only from the eighteenth century. Anything hidden there around 1615, the year Vernon wrote his poem, would probably have been removed and even destroyed.

I was now convinced that the numerals were a code, and that I had the solution. If just one or two of the verses had connected with the locality, then it might have been coincidence, but every single verse seemed to match precisely. Time and time again I kept opening the Bible at a random verse to see if I could make it fit with a location, but apart from once – even then with a stretch of the imagination – it didn't come close.

This made the entire episode all the more frustrating. Some workmen in the 1700s probably found an ancient chalice, kept it from the vicar, and sold it to the local pawnbroker for the price of a drink.

Had the Marian Chalice – the historical Grail – really been hidden in Weston parish church? The last reference in Vernon's list seemed very much to suggest so. Psalm 116, verse 13 reads:

I will take the cup of salvation, and call upon the name of the Lord.

It was not until the summer of 1994 that I realised I might have been looking in the wrong church. I was explaining the code to a friend, local librarian Jean Astle. While reading through the list and following the course I had taken on the map, Jean concluded that my trail did not fit with the instructions. The fifth verse had read:

They go up by the mountains; they go down by the valleys unto the place which thou hast founded for them.

Jean pointed out that I had only followed down a valley to reach Weston church, whereas the verse had specifically told me to 'go up by the mountains' before going 'down by the valleys'. I had assumed that the mountains referred to the White Cliff on which the ruined chapel stood. Indicating the map, Jean pointed out the mountains might refer to the high hills directly facing the end of the rocky gorge. There I had turned right, in order to continue following the valley downwards. If I had gone over the hills I would have reached another valley about a mile away, which did indeed lead to a second church, about three miles away in Hodnet. I was sure we were on to something; Hodnet parish church stands beside Hodnet Hall, the home of Robert Vernon. Moreover, Vernon was actually buried in that church. It was certainly worth a visit.

Hodnet parish church was built in the Middle Ages, but the present building is Tudor, dating from around 1550. Consequently it would have been there in Vernon's day. It had been renovated in the 1850s but these were only interior repairs. If anything had been hidden in the church walls around 1615 then it could still be there.

Entering the church, I consulted the first reference I had followed in the Weston church, Psalm 142, verse 4: 'I looked on my right hand and beheld.' I found myself looking down the church aisle towards the choir. The next reference, Psalm 123, verse 1, read: 'Unto thee lift I up mine eyes.' I raised my eyes to see a stained-glass window depicting the four Evangelists, Matthew, Mark, Luke and John. The next reference, Psalm 118, verse 22, was: 'The stone which the builders refused is become the headstone of the corner.' There was no headstone in the corner; the window covered the relevant area of the church.

In order to have the church walls electronically scanned, I acquired the help of Kerry Harper, a research graduate in archaeology at Birmingham University. She managed to borrow a device that could differentiate between varying densities in stonework; if there were any cavities in which something could have been hidden it would find them. The entire church was swept but revealed nothing.

Then, when I had just about given up hope altogether, Kerry suggested that the stained-glass window might be important. She pointed out something that I had previously taken to be coincidence. The figure of St John, situated to the extreme right of the window, and so the nearest to the relevant corner of the church, held in his hands a golden chalice. The other three Evangelists merely held books. I had previously decided that the figure could not be related to the search as it only dated from the 1850s when the church was renovated, but Kerry suggested that it might have replaced an original bearing the same image. Sadly, no record survived of the original window; however, we discovered something equally fascinating. The window had been designed and donated to the church by the Shropshire antiquarian Thomas Wright, the same man who had translated and published *Fulke le Fitz Waryn*, Vernon's *Quest of Fulk Fitz Warine*, and *Sir Gawain and the Red Knight* – the poem which had contained the code that led us to the church.

Wright lived only a few miles from Hodnet in the village of Wollerton. Although he published a number of books on Shropshire history, almost no records survive of the man himself. However, it was fairly clear why he had had such an interest in the romance of Fulk Fitz Warine and the works of Robert Vernon: his wife, Frances, was the last of the Hodnet Vernons. The Wrights had had only one child, a son, Richard, who had died in infancy. Consequently, if my conclusions were correct, having descended from Fulk Fitz Warine, Wright's son would have been the last of the Grail family.

As the edition of Vernon's poem to include the numeral code was printed by Thomas Wright, perhaps the code had been *his* addition. In other words, it had been Wright who had hidden the chalice in the 1850s, once the family line had ended. If so, then the stained-glass window –

commissioned by Wright himself – must be important. The four Evangelists: what could it mean?

The last of the Tarot trumps had shown the four evangelical symbols, the bull, the lion, the eagle and the angel, and the *Folie* romance had been based on the same symbolism as the Tarot. Was there a link? The stained-glass window even showed the four creatures above the heads of the saints. It wasn't until the spring of 1995 that I discovered that four statues depicting exactly the same evangelical symbols had once stood in a labyrinth of caves facing the Red Castle at Hawkstone Park. Again, they had been erected by Thomas Wright in the 1850s.

Beneath the arch of the ruined chapel, cut into the White Cliff, facing the Red Castle, are a series of tunnels and chambers. They were made in the 1780s by the owner of the estate, Richard Hill, who constructed a whole series of follies on his land. However, it is thought that Hill merely enlarged an already existing series of tunnels which were copper mines dating from Roman times. In 1934 Shropshire naturalist Mary Broquet described the tunnels in her book, *Shropshire Rambles*:

> The centrepiece of the labyrinth is a gallery eighty feet long, surrounded by pillars. Once the whole gallery was painted sea green, and the pillars were covered with shells. In the middle of the last century Thomas Wright, the antiquary, added to the grotto four statutes, a winged angel, a bull, a lion, and an eagle, which stood beneath the arch. The lion and the eagle have now been moved to the Red Castle, but the bull and the angel have been lost. An interesting little tale concerns one of the statutes. In 1920 Mr Wright's grandson, Walter Langham, found a tiny cup in the base of the eagle statue. It is thought to be a scent jar of some antiquity, but the reason for it being there is one of the mysteries that the present owner so loves to relate.

Wright had erected four statues depicting the evangelical symbols, and in one of them – the eagle – a *cup* had been discovered. In the stained-glass window the Evangelist St John holds a cup in his hand, and he is the Gospel writer represented by the eagle. Indeed, the eagle is actually shown above his head. Had the window been the last clue to reveal that the cup had been hidden in the eagle statue in the labyrinth? It made sense: anyone who had followed the Psalm trail in the 1920s would have seen the statues. All they had to do was make the connection. Perhaps

Walter Langham had done just that. Unfortunately, none of the statutes now survive to be examined. The last of them, the lion, was destroyed some years ago.

Mary Broquet calls Langham Wright's grandson. But Wright's only child, Richard, had died as a youngster. However, Wright's widow, Frances, remarried, and it was her daughter Edith who was Langham's mother. Since it was Frances from whom the Vernon line had descended, the blood line of the 'Grail family' had not ended after all. Remarkably, if my theory was correct, the man who found the cup in the statue was the direct descendant of Robert Vernon, Fulk Fitz Warine, Payne Peveril, and Owain Ddantgwyn – he *was* the living Grail guardian. Had he discovered the Grail? Was the cup the Marian Chalice?

The last of the line, Walter Langham's great-granddaughter, Victoria Palmer, is still alive today. The twenty-four-year-old graphic designer now lives in Rugby in Warwickshire, and she still possesses the cup found at Hawkstone Park. She had absolutely no idea of its importance, knowing only that it had been found by her ancestor, and that it was thought to be an old scent jar.

Remarkably, the artefact is only six centimetres high, with a round base and a stunted stem. Made from onyx, a semi-precious green stone, it resembles an egg cup, except that its rim is curled inwards. The reason for this, it has been suggested, is that it once had a lid. It certainly appears very old as it is worn away in places. Fascinated by our story, Victoria allowed Kerry to have the cup examined at Birmingham University. Unfortunately, there was no way of scientifically determining its age; only organic remains can be carbon-dated. Microscopy examination, however, revealed no evidence of machining, so at least it had been hand-made. Although that didn't prove that it was old, it suggested that it had probably been made before the Industrial Revolution.

Could this really be the Marian Chalice? Although legends told how the chalice was made of gold and silver, no contemporary description survives. If it had been a cup used by Mary Madgalene in the early first century, it is more likely to have been a simpler artefact, such as a stone cup. In fact, a number of stone or pottery cups of similar size and design have been discovered at archaeological excavations around the Dead Sea, and are thought to have belonged to the first-century Jewish sect the Essenes. However, more significantly, when the cup was taken to the British Museum, it was suggested that it *might* have been a Roman scent jar. Unfortunately, no one was prepared to commit themselves; it could equally have been a nineteenth-century replica. On the positive side, Kerry made an interesting suggestion. If anything had been used to contain the blood of Christ – as the Marian Chalice was believed to have done – it was more likely to have been a jar of some sort than an open cup.

Whether or not this small onyx cup really is the Marian Chalice will probably never be known. We may, however, have finally solved the age-old mystery of the Grail romances. They appear to have originated with a story written around 1100 – an allegory concerning an ostracised Christian sect, descendents of the Gnostics who claimed spiritual authority via an alternative apostolic line of succession. Because this original story concerned the lineage of King Arthur, and Arthur became a popular figure of romance in the twelfth century, other authors adopted the Grail story and adapted it to appeal to their own particular readership, seemingly having little understanding of its true significance. In conclusion, therefore, this would appear to have been the sequence of historical events which gave rise to the Grail legend we know today:

Until the early fourth century, various Chritian sects existed throughout the Roman Empire. One of these, the Gnostics, claimed to have possessed a book containing secret words of Jesus – the Gospel of Thomas. In 327, however, the emperor Constantine the Great established Catholic Christianity as the State religion of the empire and, along with other nonconforming sects, the Gnostics were outlawed. Although within a few decades Gnosticism had successfully been suppressed elsewhere in the empire, it continued in the relative isolation of Britain. Here, Gnosticism seems to have inspired the fourth-century British priest Pelagius to established a breakaway Church. Unlike the Catholics who claimed spiritual descent from St Peter, the Pelagian Church evidently claimed spiritual succession from Joseph of Arimathea.

In AD 410, when Rome was sacked by the barbarian Visigoths, the most important Christian relics were brought to the safety of Britain, to the principal city of Viroconium. The relics apparently included artefacts believed to be: the Marian Chalice which once held Jesus' blood; the plate from the Last Supper; the lance which pierced Christ's side during the Crucifixtion; and the sword used to behead John the Baptist.

When Britain broke from Roman rule in the second decade of the fifth century, the British leader Vortigern officially sanctioned Pelagianism, and the dissenting British Church refused to return the holy relics to Rome once the city had been reoccupied by the emperor Honorius. A succession of British kings continued to rule from Viroconium for some two and a half centuries, including the historical Arthur around the year 500. These rulers, who later became the Powysian kings, seemed to have remained head of the Pelagian Church, using their possession of the Roman relics to legitimise their authority. The most important of these relics, the Marian Chalice (and possibly the others), seems to have remained in the possession of the Powysian kings until their descendants became Welsh barons under the control of the conquering Normans in the eleventh century. Lynette, the granddaughter of the last Powysian king, Cadfarch, married the Norman baron Payne Peveril who had fought with William the Conqueror at the Battle of Hastings in 1066.

Around 1100, Payne Peveril's chaplain, the St Asaph monk Blayse, wrote the *Peveril*, in which he describes his master as the holder of the Grail – seemingly the Marian Chalice. Although only fragments of the *Peveril* now remain, the full story appears to have survived almost intact in a fourteenth-century translation, *La Folie Perceval*. The story concerns the spiritual descendants of Joseph of Arimathea – seemingly the Peveril family – and their role as Grail guardians, possessing the four Grail Hallows (the chalice, the sword, the plate and the lance) and the Holy Grail itself – the Gospel of Thomas. The portrayal of the Gospel of Thomas as the holiest relic, together with the inclusion of symbolism shared by the Gnostic Albigenses (in their Tarot pack), suggests that the *Peveril* was originally an allegory concerning the Peveril family inheriting the leadership of a secret Gnostic sect, presumably what remained of the Powysian Pelagian Church.

Within a few decades the *Peveril* story seems to have been copied and widely disseminated. Because the legendary King Arthur had become a popular figure of romance by the late twelfth century, and the *Peveril* included Arthur as the ancestor of the Peveril family, a number of European writers began to compose their own variations of the *Peveril* Grail story. It is unlikely that these authors understood the true significance of the original romance, as they each altered the story to suit their readership. The name Peveril was changed to Perceval and the story no longer concerned Arthur's medieval descendants, but his Dark Age contemporaries. Moreover, the Grail became different relics to different writers.

The four Grail Hallows continued to be included in most of the romances written a decade or so either side of 1200. However, the importance of the sacred Gospel was either played down or ignored altogether, presumably because reference to such a book would have been considered heresy by the powerful Catholic Church of the Middle Ages.

Around 1190 Chrétien de Troyes included all four Hallows, but concentrated on the plate as the Grail itself. Although he does not specifically say so, his Grail is almost certainly being portrayed as the plate of the Last Supper, as the Grail guardian is served a mass wafer from it. Within ten years, the First Continuation followed Chrétien's lead by making the plate a Grail, but did not portray it as the plate of the Last Supper. In this version it is made by Joseph of Arimathea specifically to collect blood from Christ's crucified body. The reason that the author chose to separate the artefact from Jesus himself was probably that he included another Grail in the story – one which he intended to have equal significance – the carved head of Jesus that could still be seen at Lucca Cathedral in Tuscany.

About 1200 Robert de Boron seems to have conflated all previous renditions of the Grail romance in his *Joseph d'Arimathie*. Seemingly influenced by the legend that the Marian Chalice had been used to collect Christ's blood, he made the Grail a cup, and influenced by Chrétien's association of the Grail with the Last Supper, he made it the original cup of Eucharist. Robert does not associate the Grail with Mary Magdalene, however, but follows the author of the First Continuation by having it being used by Joseph of Arimathea.

Unlike Chrétian and the author of the First Continuation, Robert de Boron does allude to the secret Gospel by saying how the Grail guardian, the Fisher King, is taught the secret words of Jesus. About the same time, the author of the *Didcot Perceval* also concentrated on the cup as the Holy Grail and, like Robert, alluded to the Book of the Holy Vessel by having the Fisher King instruct his successor with Jesus' secret teachings. Around 1205 the author of *Perlesvaus* seems to have attempted to remain true to the original story by potraying the Grail as a secret Gospel, while cleverly disguising the fact. He does not say what the Grail is, merely that it mysteriously reveals episodes from Christ's life – possibly hinting at a Gospel which was not included in the Bible. By 1220 the Vulgate author was brave enough to directly describe the Grail as a book, in this case a book written by Christ himself. However, he also included the by now more familiar Grail, the chalice of the Last Supper.

To confuse matters, other legends seem to have influenced the development of the Grail story: Wolfram von Eschenbach incorporated a magic stone from an Arabian source as his Grail, whereas early Welsh tales of Arthur searching for a magical cauldron seem to have been interpolated into the Arthurian saga, resulting in modern speculation concerning the Grail having originally been such a cauldron.

Around 1260 an anonymous author, someone evidently linked with the Peveril family, appears to have attempted to put the record straight concerning the origin of the Grail story. In his *Fulke le Fitz Waryn* he describes Payne Peveril's great-grandson Fulk Fitz Warine discovering the Grail in his castle at Whittington. This Grail is a cup – probably the Marian Chalice – although a more important Grail, the Book of the Holy Vessel, is also inherited by Fulk.

Although by the fourteenth century the Grail had become solely the cup of the Last Supper, we can clearly see that the word did not apply exclusively to that particular relic when the first Grail romances were composed. There were a number of Grails, and some of these have now either been found or identified, while others may be historical artefacts still awaiting discovery:

1. The Book of the Holy Vessel is without doubt the Gospel of Thomas. The only surviving copy is now in the Coptic Museum in Cairo.

2. The Marian Chalice, the cup discovered by the Empress Helena in 327, may have been the relic found and re-hidden by Fulk Fitz Warine in the mid thirteenth century. The same artefact was claimed to have been unearthed by Fulk's descendant Robert Vernon in the 1590s, and seemingly remained in the family until it was hidden at Hawkstone Park in the 1850s to be recovered by Walter Langham in 1920. The cup is now in the possession of Langham's great-granddaughter Victoria Palmer, a direct descendant of the medieval Peverils, and of Owain Ddantgwyn – the historical King Arthur.

3. The Volto Santo, the carved head of Jesus said to have been made by Nicodemus, was an historical artefact kept at Lucca Cathedral in Tuscany.

4. The relic thought to be the plate of the Last Supper, *the* Grail in Chretien's version of the story, may have been amongst the relics inherited by the Peverils in the late eleventh century. Its subsequent whereabouts, however, remain a mystery. It was not mentioned in *Fulke le Fitz Waryn* in the thirteenth century, neither was it claimed to have been discovered by Fulk's descendent Robert Vernon. Perhaps it still remains to be discovered where Fulk is said to have found the chalice, in Whittington Castle – the historical Grail castle in the medieval romances. The same may also apply to the relics believed to have been the lance of the Crucifixion and the sword which beheaded John the Baptist.

5. The Lapis Excillis, the magic stone of Wolfram von Eschenbach, was claimed to have been possessed by a number of medieval alchemists who believed that it could be used to transform base metals into gold. What happened to it, if it ever existed, is open to further investigation.

6. Although not included as a Grail in the medieval romances, certain aspects of the Grail story may have been influenced by early Welsh tales of Arthur's search for the cauldron of Di-Wrnach. If based on events associated with the historical Arthur, the cauldron in question may just possibly have been the one discovered at the Berth at Baschurch, the burial site of the Powysian kings. It is now in the British Museum.

Today the Grail is no longer simply an artefact – it has come to represent a search for truth or enlightenment. From this perspective, the present investigation has indeed proved successful. This search to discover the truth behind the Grail legend has thrown invaluable new light upon the historical King Arthur and the mystery of the medieval romances.

Summary

- In 1596 Robert Vernon purchased the site of the White Abbey, where Fulk had hidden the Grail in *Fulke le Fitz Waryn*. While renovating the abbey ruins, Vernon claimed to have made a remarkable discovery – seemingly the Grail itself. Around 1615 he composed *Sir Gawain and the Red Knight*, in which the Grail is stolen by the Red Knight and taken to the Red Castle. The Red Castle is an historical building; its red-brick ruins can still be seen at Hawkstone Park, about three miles south-west of Hodnet.

- The poem ends with Gawain hiding the Grail. Strangely, Vernon does not say where it was hidden, merely that Gawain stood on the battlements of the Red Castle contemplating its hiding place. At the end of the poem there are two lines of mysterious numerals which seem to relate to Psalm verses in the Bible. If Vernon had discovered the Grail at the White Abbey, then perhaps he had re-hidden it before his death and left the Psalm verses as a coded message to reveal its location?

- The code was found to refer to geographical locations around the Red Castle. For example, one verse includes the words, 'For thou art my rock and my fortress', seemingly referring to the Red Castle itself, and another reads, 'Lead me to the rock that is higher than I', and directly opposite the Red Castle there tower the rocks of White Cliff. Continuing in the same fashion, the instructions eventually lead to the parish church in Hodnet.

- On entering the church, the relevant verse reads, 'I looked on my right hand and beheld.' To the right of the church entrance is a stained-glass window depicting the four Evangelists, Matthew, Mark, Luke and John. The window was designed and donated to the church by Thomas Wright, the antiquarian who had published Vernon's *Sir Gawain and the Red Knight* in the 1850s. Wright's wife, Frances, was the surviving descendant of Robert Vernon.

- As the edition of Vernon's poem to include the numeral code was printed by Thomas Wright, perhaps the code had been *his* addition. If so, then the stained-glass window must be important. The window not only depicts the Evangelists, but includes the four symbols for the Gospel writers: the bull, the lion, the eagle and the angel. Remarkably, four statues depicting exactly the same evangelical symbols once stood in a labyrinth of caves cut into the White Cliff at Hawkstone Park. Again, they had been erected by Thomas Wright in the 1850s.

- In 1934 Shropshire naturalist Mary Boquet describes the finding of a small cup in the base of the eagle statue in 1920. It had been discovered by Frances Wright's grandson, Walter Langham. In the stained-glass window the Evangelist St John holds a cup in his hand, and he is the Gospel writer represented by the eagle. The window may, therefore, have been the final clue to reveal that the cup had been hidden in the eagle statue in the labyrinth.

- Today the cup is owned by Walter Langham's great-granddaughter, Victoria Palmer. The artefact is just six centimetres high, with a round base and a stunted stem. Made from onyx, a semi-precious green stone, it resembles an egg cup, except that its rim is curled inwards. The reason for this, it has been suggested, was that it once had a lid.

- When the cup was taken to the British Museum, it was suggested that it might have been a Roman scent jar. If anything had been used to contain the blood of Christ – as the Marian Chalice was believed to have done – it is more likely to have been a jar of some sort than an open cup. Whether or not this tiny cup really had been the Marian Chalice is impossible to say. However, it may well have been the relic that had remained in the Peveril family for generations – an artefact that in the medieval romances became the Holy Grail.

Chronology

43–7	Britain conquered by Emperor Claudius and becomes an island province of the Roman Empire.
380	Pelagius leaves Britain for Rome and comes into conflict with the Church.
383	Magnus Maximus proclaimed emperor by the British legions, invades Gaul and Italy but is defeated by Theodosius I.
401	Alaric, king of the Visigoths, invades Northern Italy.
408	Alaric lays siege to Rome and Emperor Honorius is forced to withdraw troops from Britain.
410	Alaric sacks Rome. Marian Chalice leaves Rome. Honorius unable to respond to the British plea for reinforcements. Last of the Roman legions leave Britain.
416	The Roman Church proclaims the teachings of Pelagius heresy.
420	Mass rebuilding of Viroconium.
429	Germanus, Bishop of Auxerre, visits Britain as an envoy of the Catholic Church.
447	Germanus' second visit to Britain.
451	Attila the Hun defeated at Chalons.
455–60	Anglo-Saxons take control of eastern Britain. Vortigern deposed.
460	Ambrosius leader of British forces. British defences reorganised.
470	British contingent fights for Emperor Anthemius in northern France.
476	Odovacer defeats Emperor Romulus Augustulus and

159

	proclaims himself King of Italy. Final collapse of the Western Roman Empire.
480	Military stalemate between the Britons and the Saxons in the south of England. The Angles suffer defeat in the north. Cunorix buried in Viroconium.
488	Hengist dies and is succeeded by Octha. Arthur succeeds Ambrosius.
488–93	The Arthurian campaigns.
493	The Battle of Badon. Anglo-Saxons retreat into south-east England.
519	Possible date for the death of Arthur. Maglocunus becomes King of Gwynedd. Cuneglasus becomes King of Powys.
530	Byzantine emperor, Justinian I, fails to recapture the Western Empire.
545	Gildas writes *On the Ruin and Conquest of Britain*.
549	Death of Maglocunus.
610	The poem *Gododdin* composed.
658	Oswy sacks Powys. Death of Cynddylan. The British lose Staffordshire and Shropshire and the Mercians occupy western Powys. Wulfhere King of Mercia.
731	Bede writes the *Ecclesiastical History of the English People*.
800	The Pope crowns Charlemagne of the Franks Holy Roman Emperor.
830	Nennius writes the *Historia Brittonum*.
850	*The Song of Llywarch the Old* is composed in its present form. Cyngen, King of Powys, erects the Pillar of Eliseg.
871–99	The *Anglo-Saxon Chronicle*, under the supervision of Alfred the Great, compiled from early monastic records.
900	*The Spoils of Annwn* is originally composed.
927	Athelstan effectively unites the Anglo-Saxon people and becomes first king of all England.
950	*Culhwch and Olwen* is originally composed.
955	The *Welsh Annals* are compiled.
1100	Possible date for the *Peveril*.
1135	*The History of the Kings of Britain* is completed by

Geoffrey of Monmouth.

1160	*The Dream of Rhonabwy* composed.
1170	Birth of Fulk Fitz Warine.
1190	Chretien de Troyes writes *Le Conte del Graal*.
1189	Accession of Richard I.
1190	The monks of Glastonbury Abbey claim to have discovered the grave of King Arthur.
1193–4	Richard I held captive in Germany.
1195	First and Second Continuations of *Le Conte del Graal* are written.
1197	Fulk Fitz Warine becomes Lord of Whittington.
1199	Accession of King John.
1200	Fulk Fitz Warine outlawed on charges of treason. Robert de Boron composes *Joseph d'Arimathie*. He introduces the theme of the Holy Grail as the vessel used by Christ at the Last Supper.
1203	The *Didcot Perceval* is composed. Fulk Fitz Warine pardoned by King John.
1205	Wolfram von Eschenbach writes his epic Arthurian story *Parzival*, in which he depicts the Grail as a magical stone.
1215	Fulk Fitz Warine joins the baronial revolt. King John signs the Magna Carta at Runnymede.
1216	Death of King John. Accession of Henry III.
1217	Fulk Fitz Warine makes peace with Henry III.
1220	Vulgate Cycle *Lancelot* and the *Queste* composed, as is *Perlesvaus*.
1256	Death of Fulk Fitz Warine.
1260	Probable date for the composition of *Fulke le Fitz Waryn*.
1264	Death of Fulk's son at the Battle of Lewes.
1265	*The Book of Aneirin* is compiled, containing the oldest surviving copy of the *Gododdin*.
1275	*The Book of Taliesin* is compiled, containing *The Spoils of Annwn*.
1322	The Lancastrian revolt.
1323	Edward II's royal progress, leading to Nottingham in November.
1325	*The White Book of Rhydderch* is compiled, containing

the earliest section from *Culhwch and Olwen.*

1330   The surviving copy of *La Folie Perceval* is written.

1377   William Langland's poem *Piers the Ploughman* mentions Robin Hood rhymes.

1400   Possible date for the composition of the *Gest. Sir Gawain and the Green Knight* composed by an anonymous writer from the north-east Midlands. *The Red Book of Hergest* is compiled, containing the *Dream of Rhonabwy*, the tale of *Culhwch and Olwen*, and the surviving copy of *The Song of Llywarch the Old.*

1420   Andrew de Wyntoun, in his *Original Chronicle of Scotland*, says that 'Little John and Robin Hood, as outlaws were renowed' in the early 1280s.

1470   Sir Thomas Malory completes *Le Morte d'Arthur*, the most famous of all Arthurian romances.

1510   *A Lyttell Geste of Robyn Hode* is published by the English printer Wynken de Worde.

1515   A second edition of the *Gest*, entitled *A Gest of Robyn Hode*, is published.

1521   Scottish writer John Major, in his *History of Greater Britain*, states that Robin was outlawed between 1193 and 1194, while Richard I, following his crusade to the Holy Land, was held captive in Germany.

1542   John Leland, Henry VIII's chief antiquarian, refers to Robin Hood as a nobleman in his *Collectanea.*

1550   Anonymous Shropshire poem *Robin and Marian* composed.

1562   Publication of Richard Grafton's *Chronicle*. Grafton claims to have discovered an 'old and authentic pamphlet' recording Robin's life as a lord, along with 'records in the Exchequer' referencing the confiscation of his lands.

1567   The surviving copy of *Diarebion Camberac*, containing the Welsh Triads, is compiled.

1598   Elizabethan playwright Anthony Munday writes *The Downfall of Robert the Earl of Huntingdon.*

1600   With Henry Chettle, Anthony Munday writes *The Death of Robert the Earl of Huntingdon*. Robert

Chronology

Vernon writes *The Quest of Fulk Fitz Warine.*
1615 Robert Vernon writes *Sir Gawain and the Red Knight.*
1852 The sub-commissioner of public records, Yorkshire antiquarian Joseph Hunter, publishes his *Mr Hunter's Critical and Historical Tracts. No IV. The Ballad Hero Robin Hood*, subtitled *Robin Hood: His Period, Real Character, Etc., Investigated and Perhaps Ascertained.*
1850 Hodnet church renovated.
1855 Thomas Wright publishes a translation of *Fulke le Fitz Waryn.* He also publishes Robert Vernon's *The Quest of Fulk Fitz Warine* and *Sir Gawain and the Red Knight.*
1920 A small cup, believed to be a Roman scent jar, discovered at Hawkstone Park.

Bibliography

Source material, in the original and in translation

The Anglo-Saxon Chronicle, trans. G. N. Garmonsway, Everyman's Library, London, 1967.

Bede, *The Ecclesiastical History of the English Nation*, trans. J. A. Giles, Everyman's Library, London, 1970.

L. T. Topsfield, *Chretien de Troyes: A Study of the Arthurian Romances*, Cambridge University Press, Cambridge, 1981 (for *Le Conte del Graal*).

The Continuations of the Old French 'Perceval', trans. William Roach, University of Pennsylvania Press, Philadelphia, 1983 (for the Continuations).

The Romance of Perceval in Prose, trans. Dell Skeels, University of Washington Press, Seattle, 1961 (for the *Didcot Perceval*).

Fulke le Fitz Waryn, trans. Thomas Wright, Warton Club, London, 1855.

Robert Vernon, *Sir Gawain and the Red Knight*, ed. Thomas Wright, Warton Club, London, 1855.

Geoffrey of Monmouth, *History of the Kings of Britain*, trans. Lewis Thorpe, Penguin, London, 1966.

The Gest of Robin Hood, ed. W. H. Clawson, Toronto University Press, Toronto, 1909.

Gildas, *On the Ruin and Conquest of Britain*, Latin & trans. Michael Winterbottom, *History from the Sources Vol. 7*, Phillimore, Chichester, 1978.

Nennius, *Historia Brittonum*, Latin and trans. John Morris, *History from the Sources Vol. 8*, Phillimore, Chichester, 1980.

Olympiodorus, *The Works of Olympiodorus*, trans. D. C. Scott, Chicago University Press, Chicago, 1952.

Perlesvaus, trans. William Nitze, Chicago University Press, Chicago, 1937.

Robert Vernon, *The Quest of Fulk Fitz Warine*, ed. Thomas Wright, Warton Club, London, 1855.

The Oxford Book of Welsh Verse in English, ed. Gwyn Jones, Oxford University Press, Oxford, 1977. Also: *The Age of Arthur*, John Morris, Phillimore, Chichester, 1977 (for *The Song of Llywarch the Old*).

Jane E. Burns, *Arthurian Fictions: Re-reading the Vulgate Cycle*, Ohio State University Press, Columbus, 1985.

Hugh D. Sacker, *An Introduction to Wolfram's 'Parzival'*, Cambridge University Press, Cambridge, 1963.

Welsh Annals, Latin and trans. John Morris, *History from the Sources Vol. 8*, Phillimore, Chichester, 1980.

The Mabinogion, trans. Gwyn Jones and Thomas Jones, Everyman's Library, London, 1975 (for *Culhwch and Olwen*, *The Dream of Rhonabwy* and *Peredur*).

Poems from the Book of Taliesin, ed. G. J. Evans, Tramvan, Llanbedrog, 1915 (for *The Spoils of Annwn*).

Joseph Clancy, *The Earliest Welsh Poetry*, Macmillan, London, 1970 (for *The Dialogue of Arthur*).

Thomas Parry, *A History of Welsh Literature*, trans. H. Idris Bell, Oxford University Press, Oxford, 1955 (for *The Triads*).

Selected Bibliography

Alcock, Leslie, *Arthur's Britain: History and Archaeology AD 376–634*, London, 1971.

Arbert, Edward (ed.), *A Transcript of the Registers of the Company of Stationers of London 1554–1640*, London, 1875.

Bibliography

Ashe Geoffrey, *The Quest for Arthur's Britain*, London, 1968.

> *Camelot and the Vision of Albion*, London, 1971.

> *A Guidebook to Arthurian Britain*, Wellingborough, 1983.

> *Avalonian Quest*, London, 1984.

> *The Discovery of King Arthur*, London, 1985.

Baildon, W. P. (ed.), *Court Rolls of the Mannor of Wakefield*, Yorkshire Archaeological Society Records Series, 1945.

> *Notes on the Religious and Secular Houses of Yorkshire*, Yorkshire Archaeological Society *Records Series, 1931.*

Barber, Richard, King Arthur in Legend and History, London, 1973.

Baugh, G. C. & Cox, D. C., *Monastic Shropshire*, Shrewsbury, 1982.

Bellamy, John, *Robin Hood: An Historical Enquiry*, London, 1985.

Benham, W. G., *Playing Cards: Their History and Secrets*, London, 1931.

Bindhoff, S. T., *Tudor England*, Harmondsworth, 1950.

Bogdanow, Fanni, *The Romance of the Grail*, Manchester, 1966.

Boulton, Helen (ed.), *The Sherwood Forest Book*, Thoroton Society Records Series, 1965.

Bradbrook, Muriel, *The Rise of the Common Player*, London, 1962.

Bronson, Bertrand, *The Traditional Tunes of the Child Ballads*, Princeton, 1966.

Brown, W. (ed.), *Yorkshire Deeds*, Yorkshire Archaeological Society Records Series, 1955.

Bryant, Frank, *A History of English Balladry*, Boston, 1913.

Camden, William, *Annales*, London, 1625.

Cavendish, Richard, *King Arthur and the Grail*, London, 1978.

167

Chadwick, Nora K., *Celtic Britain*, New York, 1963.

> *The Age of the Saints in the Early Celtic Church*, London, 1981.

> *The Celts*, Harmondsworth, 1970.

Chambers, E. K., *English Literature at the Close of the Middle Ages*, Oxford, 1945.

> *The Elizabethan Stage*, Oxford, 1923.

> *The English Folk Play*, Oxford, 1933.

> *Oxford Book of Sixteenth-Century Verse*, Oxford, 1961.

Child, Francis J. (ed.), *The English and Scottish Popular Ballads*, New York, 1956.

Clancy, Joseph, *Pendragon: Arthur and his Britain*, London, 1971.

Clawson, W. H., *The Gest of Robin Hood*, Toronto, 1909.

Comfort, W. W., *Arthurian Romances*, New York, 1914.

Copley, Gordon K., *The Conquest of Wessex in the Sixth Century*, London, 1954.

Crossley-Holland, Kevin, *British Folk Tales*, London, 1987.

Davidson, H. E., *Gods and Myths in Northern Europe*, Harmondsworth, 1964.

Delaney, Frank, *Legends of the Celts*, London, 1989.

Dillon, Myles & Chadwick, Nora K., *The Celtic Realms*, New York, 1967.

Dodson, R. B. & Tylor, J., *Rymes of Robin Hood*, London, 1976.

Dugdale, William, *Antiquities of Warwickshire*, London, 1656.

Dunning, Robert, *Arthur – King in the West*, London, 1988.

Empson, William, *Some Verses of Pastoral*, London, 1935.

Bibliography

Fife, Graham, *Arthur the King*, London, 1990.

Ford, Patrick, *The Mabinogi and Other Medieval Welsh Tales*, Los Angeles, 1977.

Frere, S., *Britannia*, London, 1967.

Fryde, N., *The Tyranny and Fall of Edward II*, Cambridge, 1979.

Fuller, Thomas, *The History of the Worthies of England*, London, 1662.

Gable, J. H., *Bibliography of Robin Hood*, Lincoln (Nebraska), 1939.

Garmonsway, G. N. (trans.), *The Anglo-Saxon Chronicle*, London, 1967.

Gerould, Gordon, *The Ballad of Tradition*, New York, 1932.

Giles, J. A., (ed.), *The Ecclesiastical History of the English Nation* (trans. from Bede), London, 1970.

Goetinck, Glenys, *Peredur: A Study of Welsh Tradition in the Grail Legends*, Cardiff, 1975.

Grafton, Richard, *Grafton's Chronicle*, London, 1809.

Green, Miranda, *The Gods of the Celts*, Gloucester, 1986.

Hales, J. W. & Furnivall, F. J., *Bishop Percy's Folio Manuscript*, London, 1868.

Harding, A., *The Law Courts of Medieval England*, London, 1973.

Hargrave, Catherine, *A History of Playing Cards*, New York, 1966.

Harris, P. V., *The Truth About Robin Hood*, Mansfield, 1973.

Hart, D. F., *The Legend of Pope Joan*, London, 1966.

Hodgkin, R. H., *A History of the Anglo-Saxons: Vol. 1*, London, 1952.

A History of the Anglo-Saxons: Vol. 2, London, 1952.

Holt, J. C., *Robin Hood*, London, 1991.

Hunter, Joseph, *The Ballad Hero: Robin Hood*, London, 1852.

Jarman, A. O. H. & Hughes, Gwilym Rees, *A Guide to Welsh Literature*, Swansea, 1976.

Jewell, H. M. (ed.), *The Court Rolls of the Mannor of Wakefield*, Yorkshire Archaeological Society Records Series, 1982.

Keen, Maurice, *The Outlaws of Medieval Legend*, Toronto, 1961.

King, Francis, *Ritual Magic in England*, London, 1970.

Lacy, Norris (ed.), *The Arthurian Encyclopedia*, London, 1988.

Langland, William, *Piers Plowman* (ed. W. Skeat), London, 1886.

Leland, John, *The Itinerary of John Leland* (ed. Lucy Toulmin Smith), London, 1909.

Loomis, Roger Sherman, *Arthurian Literature in the Middle Ages*, Oxford, 1959.

The Grail: From Celtic Myth to Christian Symbol, London, 1993.

Wales and the Arthurian Legend, Cardiff, 1966.

McGrath, Patrick, *Papists and Puritans under Elizabeth I*, London, 1967.

Markale, Jean, *King Arthur: King of Kings*, London, 1977.

Morris, John (ed.), *The Age of Arthur: Vol. 1*, Chichester, 1977.

The Age of Arthur: Vol. 2, Chichester, 1977.

The Age of Arthur: Vol. 3, Chichester, 1977.

Owen, D. D. R., *The Evolution of the Grail Legend*, London, 1968.

Painter, S., *The Reign of King John*, Baltimore, 1952.

Page, W. (ed.), *Victoria County History, Nottinghamshire*, London, 1906.

Parry, Thomas, *A History of Welsh Literature*, (trans. H. Idris Bell), Oxford, 1955.

Percy, Thomas, *Reliques of Ancient English Poetry*, London, 1765.

Phillips, Graham & Keatman, Martin, *King Arthur: The True Story*, London, 1992.

Pollard, Alfred, *The Romance of King Arthur*, London, 1979.

Salway, Peter, *The Frontier People of Roman Britain*, Cambridge, 1965.

Sinclair, Andrew, *The Sword and the Grail*, London, 1993.

Stephens, Meic (ed.), *The Oxford Companion to the Literature of Wales*, Oxford, 1986.

Thomas, Charles, *Britain and Ireland in Early Christian Times*, London, 1971.

Thomas, W. J., (ed.), *Early English Prose Romance*, London, 1858.

Thomson, E. A., *A History of Attila and the Huns*, Oxford, 1948.

Treharne, R. F., *The Glastonbury Legends*, London, 1967.

Thorpe, Lewis (ed.), *History of the Kings of Britain* (trans. from Geoffrey of Monmouth), London, 1966.

Topsfield, L. T., *Chretien de Troyes: A Study of the Arthurian Romances*, Cambridge, 1981.

Walker, J. W., *The True History of Robin Hood*, Wakefield, 1973.

Westwood, Jennifer, *Albion: A Guide to Legendary Britain*, London, 1987.

Whitelock, Dorothy (ed.), *English Historical Documents: 500–1042*, London, 1955.

Wiles, David, *The Early Plays of Robin Hood*, Cambridge, 1981.

Wilson, R. M., *The Lost Literature of Medieval England*, London, 1952.

Williams, A. H., *An Introduction to the History of Wales*, Cardiff, 1962.

Winterbottom, Michael (ed.), *De Excidio Britanniae: History from the Sources Vol. 7* (trans. from Gildas), Chichester, 1978.

Wyntoun, Andrew, *The Original Chronicle of Andrew de Wyntoun* (ed. F. J. Amours), Edinburgh, 1907.

Index

175